Breakfast
with God

Volume 4

Also available from HarperCollins*Publishers:*

Breakfast with God Volume 1 Duncan Banks
Breakfast with God Volume 2 Gerard Kelly
Breakfast with God Volume 3 Roz Stirling

Breakfast with God

Volume 4

Simon Hall

Marshall Pickering
An Imprint of HarperCollins*Publishers*

Marshall Pickering is an Imprint of
HarperCollins*Religious*
part of HarperCollins*Publishers*
77–85 Fulham Palace Road, London W6 8JB
www.christian-publishing.com

First published in Great Britain in 2001 by Marshall Pickering

1 3 5 7 9 10 8 6 4 2

Unless otherwise indicated, scripture quotations are taken from the *Comtemporary English Version Bible*, © American Bible Society 1991, 1992, 1995.

Scripture quotations marked 'NIV' are taken from the *Holy Bible, New International Version*, © 1973, 1978, 1984 by International Bible Society. Used by permission of Hodder & Stoughton Ltd, a member of the Hodder Headline Plc Group. All rights reserved. 'NIV' is a trademark of International Bible Society. UK trademark number 1448790.

A catalogue record for this book is available from the British Library.

ISBN 0 551 03261 8

Printed and bound in Great Britain by
Martins the Printers, Berwick upon Tweed

Doing *Breakfast with God* is the greatest nourishment we could hope for each day of our lives. Simon has very helpfully laid out meals for us to munch at as we look to enjoy God and harness each day for his purposes in our lives.

MATT BIRD, DIRECTOR OF JOSHUA GENERATION

I love the idea of browsing for spiritual nuggets… It's so suitable for young adults rejecting a one-size-fits-all authoritarian approach … Packs more discipleshipping punch in amongst the eclectic references and titbits. Excellent.

GEOFFREY STEVENSON, DIRECTOR, CENTRE FOR CHRISTIAN COMMUNICATION, DURHAM

Breakfast with God is funny, flexible, friendly, deep, and full of the Bible. Simon Hall offers a varied diet of truth and honesty for the hungry disciple.

PETE WARD, LECTURER IN YOUTH MINISTRY AND THEOLOGICAL EDUCATION, KING'S COLLEGE

INTRODUCTION

Welcome to *Breakfast with God 4*. I have one page to introduce you to its many delights. As you'll see, each page of this book offers you a huge buffet breakfast of great variety. If, like me, you don't often get to stay in a swanky hotel, you will make sure that you eat every single morsel on offer, and then come back for more.

That's what I recommend, but I'm also aware that some of you are reading this on the bus, in the bath, at your workstation … and that you will need to pick carefully which choice dainties will feed you for the rest of the day. That's fine – indeed, it's why the *BWG* books are designed the way they are. However, I do suggest that you start with the Orange Juice, because everything grows out of that (not literally – I think I've overstepped the limits of my metaphor here!).

If this was a movie, you would expect this to be the fourth-best film in the series, with me, the director, being an unknown who has previously worked only on adverts and music videos. Well, *BWG* is different from movies in that this book isn't a sequel to anything: you are about to get into something that is very much its own thing. Well, it's my thing, to be exact. Reading this book, you will have a previously unavailable opportunity to roam around my mind, discovering what makes me laugh, cry, get angry, think. You will discover my little obsessions, and my big obsession: Jesus.

Of course I want you to like me: there's quite a bit of me on show. However, what I really want is for you to see something of God in here and to say, maybe even under your breath, 'Yessss!'

Orange Juice

Some other guests started saying to one another, 'Who is this who dares to forgive sins?' But Jesus told the woman, 'Because of your faith, you are now saved. May God give you peace!'

LUKE 7:49–50

The Big Breakfast

One word that Christians use to describe themselves is 'saved'. You know the old joke: 'Jesus saves, but [insert name of famous footballer here] heads in the rebound.' But what on earth does it mean to be saved? The word the Bible uses is sözö, which means a lot more than just being safe.

Jesus had an amazing ability to annoy people who thought they had God all sorted out. He was always bursting people's bubbles, particularly when they put themselves between ordinary people and God. For example, take the occasion when Jesus was at a party held for him and a load of important people by Simon, a local religious leader. In came this woman – obviously no one had even bothered to find out her name – and started pouring perfume on his feet and kissing them. Something about her attitude to Jesus led him to tell her that her sins were forgiven, that she was 'saved'.

Sometimes we hang onto the wrong thing to try to get us 'saved'. Often it's things like going to church, believing the right things and so on, but Jesus saw faith in this woman's worship. Her humble adoration of Jesus made her 'safe'.

Continental

What was it about that woman that made Jesus say, 'wherever the good news is told all over the world, people will remember what she has done' (Matthew 26:13)?

Coffee

'You believe there is only one God. That's fine. Even demons believe this, and it makes them shake with fear' (James 2:19). Faith in Jesus is trust in, and worship of, God's only Son. Take time out for an attitude check.

Orange Juice

Just then a woman … came up behind him and touched the edge of his cloak. She said to herself, 'If I only touch his cloak, I will be healed.' Jesus turned and saw her. 'Take heart, daughter,' he said, 'your faith has healed you.'

MATTHEW 9:20–22 NIV

WHOLENESS

The Big Breakfast

I once had a friend who got an unusual package from abroad. A certain preacher had sent him a handkerchief, sealed in a plastic bag and marked with the words, 'Only to be opened in case of emergency'. This handkerchief had apparently been blessed and was available for use when my friend needed a miracle. If the plastic packaging was opened, the blessing would be lost, the spiritual freshness dissipated. I wish I was joking, because such an idea is profoundly silly and conflicts with my idea of how the world works.

Yet here we are with a story about a woman who gets healed by touching Jesus' cloak. How offensive that is to my rational sensibilities. What does Jesus say to this woman? 'Don't be so superstitious, you stupid girl?' Nope. He uses exactly the same phrase as in yesterday's Bible passage – it's just the translators who insert the word 'healed' instead of 'saved'. But it does give us another clue as to what God's idea of salvation might be about. It seems that salvation might include the whole person, not just their soul or spirit …

Continental

It's often said that most Western Christians separate the 'sacred' and the 'secular', whereas the Bible doesn't make this distinction and treats the whole world as one – as God's.

Coffee

If our salvation covers the whole of life, not just 'the spiritual bit', that makes a big difference to all kinds of stuff – our lifestyle choices, our home life, our work … Is there anything in your own life which you have separated off from God? What do you need to do about it?

Orange Juice

Everyone will hate you because of me. But if you remain faithful until the end, you will be saved.

MATTHEW 10:22

SAFE DESPITE THE DANGER

The Big Breakfast

Jesus was a master at saying stuff that people knew was true but didn't want to hear. But he isn't the type to say, 'I told you so' when we try to avoid the truth and mess up. This little verse is in the middle of a big speech about what life is going to be like for the fledgling church: everyone was going to be persecuted and even kicked out of their own homes.

What's interesting, though, is that Jesus is again talking about being saved or safe. The disciples might have asked, 'So we're going to be put in prison, tortured, beaten, executed and despised, and you still want to describe us as being safe (sözö)?' There is so much of Jesus' teaching that has a 'now but not yet' quality to it, and this seems to include his teaching about salvation. He seems to be saying, 'Even though you have a tough life, if you stick at it for me, one day you will know wholeness in every area of your life.'

Trusting God is not an option for a Christian: hope for the future is central. 1 Corinthians 13 may say that love is the most important thing that 'remains', but we shouldn't forget that faith and hope are up there as well! Hope is the power to believe that God can change the future, the ability to know that you are safe in his hands.

Continental

If nobody hates you because you're a Christian, are you doing anything wrong?

Coffee

Trusting God for the future can be hard sometimes. Talk to God about something in the future that's troubling you, and take time to see if he wants to reply.

Orange Juice

When the disciples heard this, they were greatly surprised and asked, 'How can anyone ever be saved?' Jesus looked straight at them and said, 'There are some things that people cannot do, but God can do anything.'

MATTHEW 19:25–26

SALVATION: HARD OR EASY?

The Big Breakfast

Another of those rather annoying hard sayings of Jesus. He's just been talking about rich men getting into the Kingdom, camels and the eye of a needle.

I once heard that there was a gate in Jerusalem that was so narrow that it was called 'The Needle's Eye'. It was so narrow, in fact, that a trader coming through the gate would have to take all his baggage off the camel in order to get it through …

Whether or not this is true, the disciples react as one by saying, 'So what do we do, then? Just 'cos Cliff Richard's got a Rolls, does that mean he can't get into heaven?'

Jesus responds by saying something frightening: God can break the rules, maybe even his own rules. Because he wants everyone to be saved (see 1 Timothy 2:4), he can make it possible for us to be saved despite our own sinfulness. So, big cars and cheesy singles notwithstanding, Cliff is a friend of God – saved – because he trusts in God to forgive him.

Many of us, just like the Pharisees, want to make our own rules about 'who's in and who's out'. I, for one, am profoundly grateful to God that his love and salvation stretch out beyond any rule and grab me wherever I am, whatever I'm doing.

Continental

If there's anything in your life that you feel bars you from God's presence, YOU'RE WRONG! The Bible says all you need to do is turn away from it and ask God's forgiveness and help. If you feel that God likes you because of something you've done, YOU'RE WRONG TOO! Being saved is all down to God.

Coffee

Why not take a moment to thank God for the one unique thing about Christianity: you're saved not because of something you did, but because of something God did.

Orange Juice

So you will be saved, if you honestly say, 'Jesus is Lord', and if you believe with all your heart that God raised him from death.

ROMANS 10:9

CAN IT BE THIS EASY?

The Big Breakfast

Imagine you are a Christian man in the Roman Empire, circa AD 50. Every man in the Empire has to serve in the army at one point, and as part of your induction there is a quasi-spiritual ritual to go through. It's a bit like MPs in the UK declaring their allegiance to the Crown or American school-kids saluting the US flag. Only there's one problem: you have to acknowledge that Caesar – the Emperor – is a god and that you will worship him as 'Lord'. The alternative is a horrible death.

But you are a Christian, and you believe that there is only one Lord, Yahweh, the great I AM. Worshipping Caesar would be idolatry, a sin against God. Well, what would you do? Would you confess with your mouth, 'Jesus is Lord', or would you mumble away with your fingers crossed, hoping that you won't get them chopped off?

Shouting out 'Jesus is Lord!' in the safety of your bedroom isn't much of an acid test. Try shouting it in the local shopping centre. On second thoughts, don't – you'll embarrass everyone, including other Christians, probably. Why not try living in a way that shows that Jesus is the Lord of your life?

Continental

The Bible includes an ongoing debate about whether anything we do gets us into heaven. The clear answer is 'No', but if God really has saved us, then it should be obvious in the way we live our lives.

Coffee

Talk to God about how you would feel if you were a Roman and had to choose between Caesar and Jesus. Be honest with God about your fears and weaknesses, and leave space for him to speak to you.

Orange Juice

… the Lord appeared to Abram and promised, 'I will give this land to your family for ever.'

GENESIS 12:7

GOD'S LAND

The Big Breakfast

Over the next five days I'm not going to be doing *Farming for Young Christians*. What I *am* going to be doing is looking at what the Bible says about the land, the place where we live.

Many of us live in cities nowadays and we are hopelessly out of touch with the land, but in Jesus' day everyone was tied into what was going on in the land – the seasons, the agricultural calendar, the weather … To be in touch with the land is not to be a tree-hugger, it is to be a biblical Christian.

The connection between the people of Israel and the land began even before Israel had been born. Abram (later called Abraham) was promised the land of Palestine as part of the first covenant between God and Abram's descendants. Right from the beginning, God's plan didn't just involve people, it involved the land they were living in as well.

I can already hear the chorus of 'So what?'s echoing around the globe, so I will try to answer your question. My answer is this: the good of God's people is connected to the good of the land that they live in. God's promises to us include a promise that we will live in the land, and that implies a relationship with that land. So what does that mean for us?

Continental

'Everyone will find rest beneath their own fig trees or grape vines, and they will live in peace. This is a solemn promise of the Lord All-Powerful' (Micah 4:4).

Coffee

Think about the place where you live. Can you see God there? If you can, thank him for his involvement in your community. If you can't, ask him for eyes to see what he's up to, because he *is* there.

Orange Juice

…all of you who can serve in our army must pick up your weapons and lead the men of the other tribes across the River Jordan. They are your relatives, so you must help them …

JOSHUA 1:14

TAKING THE LAND

The Big Breakfast

This particular verse comes from a story that has a cool message: although the tribes of Reuben, Gad and Manasseh have been given land on the east side of the River Jordan, Joshua calls them to help the other tribes take the main land of Palestine. 'You guys are OK,' says Joshua, 'but that's because the other tribes have helped you get here. Now it's your turn.' Like most of God's people, these tribes tended to care only about their own bit of land. In contrast, God wanted the tribes to care about the *whole* land, because each tribe belonged to the others and all the tribes belonged to one family.

There's a video doing the rounds all over the world at the moment called *Transformations*. It tells the stories of four different churches around the globe where God has changed not just lives, but entire communities and economies – even the agriculture of a whole valley! Of all the things that the people on the video say, the most unforgettable thing for me is a comment by the leader of one of these amazing churches: 'I'm not going to be held accountable to God for how successful my church is, but for how I pastored my city.' Oh boy.

Continental

'Our task is a world task. It cannot be divided into the artificial compartments of "home" and "foreign".'
(John Decker).

Coffee

Is there a Christian or a church known to you that you could pray for today? So often we pray only for ourselves and our own. Why not call down a blessing from heaven on a land that you never visit?

Orange Juice

Wherever they went, my name was disgraced, because foreigners insulted my people by saying I had forced them out of their own land.

EZEKIEL 36:20

STRANGERS IN A STRANGE LAND

The Big Breakfast

The exile of God's people is probably the most significant moment in the history of Israel.

Perhaps even more than the lives of Abraham, Moses or David, the exile was a crucial turning-point. Why was it so important? Because they lost the land. The most shameful thing about being in exile was not the slavery, the poverty, the suffering – it was having been kicked out of the land.

Because we Christians are always in a minority, we tend to shy away from praying for our land, and instead we pray for the Church to be blessed. This is not a biblical prayer! Our job is to seek the success of the people and the land, and the Church is merely a vehicle for that.

I once read a book about a 'revival church' in the USA, but soon discovered that most of the growth in the church had come from Christians just moving churches and that the community where the church was situated was relatively untouched. There's something wrong there, as if the land has rejected the community of God.

As followers of Jesus we need to love the land and the people, not just those who agree with us. This is the big challenge for us in a post-Christian world.

Continental

'Think about it! Those first disciples of Christ weren't immersed in Roman culture nine to five with a house church on the weekend. No dualistic, compartmentalized faith for them. They understood that following Christ was a whole life proposition' (Tom Sine).

Coffee

How can you love your neighbourhood more?

Orange Juice

…if my people, who are called by my name, will humble themselves and pray … then will I hear from heaven and will forgive their sin and will heal their land.

2 CHRONICLES 7:14 NIV

THE RETURN

The Big Breakfast

I once saw a biker motoring down a road with this verse written on the back of his leather jacket in studs. It must have weighed a ton! Still, it is a great verse, the kind that really gets people praying. But what for? How many people realize that this verse is about the land getting healed? It's as if there's a special part of our brain that processes bits of the Bible that are too hard (miracles, anything about money, etc.) and sort of calms them down. This is one such verse: we get the bit about praying and that it leads to something good, but we ignore the fact that this verse is specifically about dealing with famine and plague in the land.

Still, it's good to realize that God takes seriously the needs of the land. Here in the UK, the land is quite a big issue, with a raging debate about genetically modified food and an active Green movement, but Christians are generally very quiet about these issues. I don't really know why.

There is clearly a challenge here for us to pray for our land – not just as the place where you live, but as something in itself. It all sounds a little bit – dare I say it? – New Age, but in an era where capitalism and industrialization have ripped us out of our environment, maybe we need to get back to nature a bit, eh?

Continental

The laws, life and beauty of the material part of God's creation are as eternal and sacred as virtue and praise are in the spiritual realms.

Coffee

Jesus told us to pray for our daily bread. Pray today for the land that grows your food, and for those who bring it to you in such wonderful condition.

Orange Juice

But the Holy Spirit will come upon you and give you power. Then you will tell everyone about me in Jerusalem, in all Judea, in Samaria, and everywhere in the world.

ACTS 1:8

THE MISSION

The Big Breakfast

We all know the story about Pentecost – flames, wind and tongues – but sometimes we forget why God did it. Well, here's what Jesus said: we are to tell everyone about him *everywhere in the world*. But that's what we send missionaries for, isn't it? So we don't have to worry about all those billions of people who don't know Jesus, do we…?

Unfortunately Jesus never said, 'Peter, James and John, you're going to Kenya and the rest of you can stay at home.' Nope, he said *everyone* would be his witnesses, and they were. After AD 70, the church in Jerusalem was scattered throughout the Roman Empire and beyond. All the Christians would have had to give an account of themselves, because their strange beliefs meant they would not worship the emperor.

And what happened? The more they got thrown to the lions, the more people joined them. Makes you think something might be missing nowadays, doesn't it? I don't know exactly what's missing, but I do know that things would change if Christians would start going where God wants them to go and simply be witnesses to what Jesus has done in their lives.

Continental

'Jesus commands us to go. It should be the exception if you stay' (Keith Green).

Coffee

Is there anywhere God wants you to go? It doesn't have to be Africa; it could be a quick visit to a lonely neighbour. Is there anyone you need to talk to about Jesus? You don't have to understand really deep theology, you just have to be able to talk about your friend Jesus.

Orange Juice

We are not fighting against humans. We are fighting against forces and authorities and against rulers of darkness and powers in the spiritual world.

EPHESIANS 6:12

GET THE PERSPECTIVE RIGHT

The Big Breakfast

Over the next five days we're going to be looking at Paul's advice on prayer in Ephesians. Sometimes the prayer described here is called 'spiritual warfare', which is fine by me – although to imagine that there are some kinds of prayer that *aren't* spiritual warfare seems a bit wrong-headed to me. Whenever we get involved with God in his business, we're involving ourselves in the struggle. And who is the struggle against? Not your boss, nor a nosey neighbour, nor the person who picks on you for being a Christian. When people sin against us, we need to remember Jesus' words on the cross: 'Father, forgive these people! They don't know what they're doing' (Luke 23:34).

Maybe you think this is all too *X-Files*. Maybe the idea of all kinds of weird creatures flying around all over the place is beyond your threshold of belief. Well, tough. Just imagine I'm talking about ideas rather than actual beings, but always remember the message: people are not our enemies and never will be. We are to turn the other cheek, to bless those who curse us. This is a radical message, one that will get you into trouble.

Continental

Why is it that the neo-Marxists are the ones with a band called 'Rage Against the Machine' and it takes Chuck D of Public Enemy to tell us to 'Fight the Powers That Be'?

Coffee

At the beginning of these five days of looking at prayer, why not start by spending some time remembering the good things that God has done for you: that in itself is an act of spiritual warfare.

Orange Juice

Be ready! Let the truth be like a belt around your waist, and let God's justice protect you like armour. Your desire to tell the good news about peace should be like shoes on your feet.

EPHESIANS 6:14–15

THE ARMOUR

The Big Breakfast

Paul starts to talk about 'the armour of God', and this is where you switch off, right? If you've grown up in the church, then you probably know this bit off by heart, and your mum has a picture of a Roman soldier in a draw somewhere, the poor guy wielding a ten-foot 'Sword of the Spirit', used in your imagination for killing dinosaurs.

Well, given that this bit is topped and tailed with comments about prayer, I'm going to interpret the armour as help on how to pray. If you tried yesterday's 'Coffee' section, then you've already begun to use truth as a weapon of spiritual warfare. Telling the world that God is great is a powerful tonic for you and drives the enemy mad!

If you were to actually live what you believe and pray that God would give you opportunities to do the right thing today, the battle would be half over. You would just need to pray for the ability to see what the Father is doing and to follow him – what Paul calls 'readiness'.

Praising God is a great place to start in prayer, but how often do you pray for readiness and righteousness? Yep, me too. I'm resolving to pray differently as I write this.

Continental

One of the characters in the film *The Matrix* says, 'It's the difference between knowing the way and walking the way.' Prayer is about your life with God, the day ahead and all your futures. *Never* let your prayer life get divorced from the rest of your life.

Coffee

Pray for readiness to do right today: 'God, I want to see what you're doing and work with you, just like Jesus did. When I go to bed tonight, I want to know that you've answered this prayer.'

Orange Juice

Let your faith be like a shield, and you will be able to stop all the flaming arrows of the evil one.

EPHESIANS 6:16

YOU GOTTA HAVE FAITH

The Big Breakfast

Oh, it's such a slippery word, 'faith'. I know the picture with the cuddly kitten and the motto, 'Faith isn't faith until it's all you're holding onto.' And I know the bit in the last Indiana Jones movie where he has to step out onto what appears to be nothing, but is in fact a computer-effects bridge (smart people, these Knights Templar).

Sometimes an organization will have a 'statement of faith' that lists a whole load of stuff that you have to believe in order to be a Christian. I don't want to say that these things don't matter, just that believing certain things and having faith are different.

Faith is about how we respond to the voices in our head that say, 'You can't do that, you'll make a fool of yourself. You'll get hurt. God will let you down. You can't trust him. You're useless, anyway – why do you think *you* can do it? You can't even sort out your own life! Just give up…'

How do you respond to those voices? Most people in this world listen to them, and give up on life before it's even started. Our job is to reject these 'flaming arrows of the evil one' and to step out into the unknown. Whoaaa!

Continental

In his book *Life after God*, Douglas Coupland has a character commenting on some blind people asking him to take their photograph. 'They couldn't see, but they still believed in sight,' he says. 'I think that's a pretty cool attitude.'

Coffee

Is there an area in your life where you need to step out in faith?

Orange Juice

Let God's saving power be like a helmet, and for a sword use God's message that comes from the Spirit.

EPHESIANS 6:17

THE FIGHT

The Big Breakfast

I live in Leeds, and up here in the cold, frosty north, somebody thought it would be a good idea to house all the stuff from the Tower of London that nobody gets to see. So, we have a huge grey building called 'The Royal Armouries' in which people run around in medieval armour and pretend to chop each other's heads off. Obviously just the right kind of entertainment for us northern savages.

I must admit it's not really my cup of tea, although I have been known to decapitate the odd orc on my computer. What I have become aware of, though, is the significance of a knight's helmet and sword. The helmet was a sign of his place in the pecking order: the fancier the helmet, the more noble its wearer. Likewise with the sword: Excalibur was a sword which could be wielded only by a king.

So these two things tell us something about our identity: we are sons of the King and we have the best weapon available to us. What is that weapon? The word of God. Now, I know that we all immediately assume that means the Bible, but that isn't the case. The Bible is *part* of the word of God, and he continues to speak to us today. Keep listening – it's your best weapon!

Continental

'What God has said isn't only alive and active! It is sharper than any double-edged sword. His word can cut through our spirits and souls and through our joints and marrow, until it discovers the desires and thoughts of our hearts' (Hebrews 4:12).

Coffee

Prayer is as much about listening as it is about talking. Either spend a few minutes in quiet or read a Psalm, and allow God's word to soak into you.

Orange Juice

Never stop praying, especially for others. Always pray by the power of the Spirit. Stay alert and keep praying for God's people.

EPHESIANS 6:18

YOU AND ME ALWAYS, AND FOREVER...

The Big Breakfast

A friend of mine has just come back from Wales, where he has been praying with Christians there who want to see God do more in their country. One of the things he said when he came back was, 'I used to think that all this "praying without ceasing" thing wasn't really real, but this week I've just begun to touch that.'

I was curious, so I asked him what it was like. 'Oh, nothing too special,' he said as he smiled at me. 'Just feeling like God was with me all the time, so it made sense to talk to him about everything.'

You may be reading this book while on a silent retreat in an ancient monastery, but I suspect you're more likely to be on a bus, sitting on the loo, or just coming out of unconsciousness as you struggle to get out of bed. If that's you, then don't despair: you can still 'stay alert'. Prayer *can* be conversations with friends, listening to beautiful music or even watching TV. Just take time every morning to remember that God is with you wherever you go, and imagine he's right next to you through the day. It might start as a discipline, but it can become completely 'normal'!

Continental

Prayer is to the spirit what food is to the body: stop eating, and you will eventually die, for sure. But something strange happens on the way: stop eating for long enough, and you lose your appetite. You only get it back when you are actually dying. How hungry for God are you?

Coffee

Plan to pray somewhere new today. Perhaps while you sit on the bus to work you could pray for the people around you. Perhaps you could sit at your computer and write a prayer on it. Perhaps you could get out into a park at lunchtime and thank God for the beauty in the world. Praying in new places reminds us that God lives there too.

Orange Juice

One day, Jacob was cooking some stew, when Esau came home hungry and said, 'I'm starving to death! Give me some of that red stew at once!' ... Jacob replied, 'Sell me your rights as the firstborn son.' **GENESIS 25:29–31**

THE TERRIBLE TWINS

The Big Breakfast

Jacob, poor soul, is probably most famous as the guy who bought Joseph his amazing technicolour dreamcoat. When I watched Dickie Attenborough play the role of Jacob in the 'family musical' about the Egyptian slave made good, I thought, 'Stupid old duffer', as I was meant to. Well, Jacob had a life of his own, much of which explains the whole Joseph-as-favourite thing.

Jacob was the younger of twins, his brother Esau being the older and stronger of the two. In Jacob's day, being older and stronger meant a lot more than it does today: Esau was the one who went out and did most of the farming work that kept the family going. Jacob was more of a thinking type, and his thoughts were not always particularly nice. He stole his brother's birthright by exploiting his hunger. Esau was so hungry after a day's work that he ended up promising the world – his entire inheritance as the firstborn son. Still, let's face it: Esau obviously didn't value his place in the family that much. So here's Jacob: he's a cheat and a social climber. Whatever next?

Continental

'We don't call it sin today – we call it self-expression' (Baroness Stocks).

Coffee

Are you looking to rise to the top at the expense of others? Trying to do your best is one thing, but are you hoping that others will fail? Are there any family members who you have fallen out with or feel competitive about? What do you need to do to sort that out?

Orange Juice

'Go and kill two of your best young goats and bring them to me. I'll cook the tasty food that your father loves so much. Then you can take it to him, so he can eat it and give you his blessing before he dies.' ***GENESIS 27:9–10***

SUNSET BEACH, PALESTINE

The Big Breakfast

Oh dear. Jacob has got his brother's word on the inheritance, but he'll never get his dad Isaac to agree to it. So his mum (now there's a *whole* other story!) hatches the plan above.

If you know this story, you'll know the whole 'hair' thing, in which Jacob has to cover himself in sheepskin to feel and smell more like his burly farmer brother – but that's really just the technical details. The key here is that Jacob is lying to his dad to get the family blessing. What a way to start! Now who remembers a story about a son who blows his inheritance? It's all as clichéd as an episode of a Channel 5 soap.

Now here's a question: what was so special about this blessing anyway? In the world we live in today, the idea that words have spiritual power seems to be very out of date. We know about the power of advertising, so why do we ignore the power of blessing and cursing? So much of what makes us comes from things that have been said to us, good or bad. Perhaps we should allow ourselves to get back into using the power of words for God.

Continental

'Lying is a leech that has sucked truth dry' (Max Frisch).

Coffee

Is there someone you could bless today? Have you ever 'cursed' someone and never apologized? Do you feel like there is a curse hanging over you? If so, ask God to break its power – he can!

Orange Juice

God will bless you, my son ... Nations will be your servants and bow down to you. You will rule over your brothers, and they will kneel at your feet.

GENESIS 27:28-29

THE BLESSING

The Big Breakfast

So here it is, what we've all been waiting for. Isaac passes on the blessing he has received from God to his son (he still thinks it's Esau). What does this great inheritance consist of?

To begin with, there is a blessing of the earth, so that Jacob may experience a life of productivity and plenty. Then the blessing is about Jacob/Esau's place in the family: the blessed son is definitely going to be the boss of the family business, no question. Finally, the blessed one is going to be looked after by God: those that curse him will be cursed, and those that bless him will be blessed. That ain't such a bad approach to life...

But stealing a blessing that doesn't belong to him is not exactly a good idea. Eventually Esau returns to his dad, who breaks the news to him that his fatherly blessing has been passed on to the wrong guy. Ouch! Not surprisingly, Esau goes ape and Jacob is gone before there's even a chance of a fight.

Maybe we can glean from this blessing what a parent is meant to hand on to a child: the skills to make a living, a sense of their place in the family, an understanding of how they fit into the moral universe. Well, maybe.

Continental

The tradition of blessing tells us this: everything that we do, everything that we say, everything that we think, makes spiritual ripples that only God sees clearly.

Coffee

Pray this ancient Celtic prayer for blessing: 'God with me protecting,/ The Lord with me directing,/ The Spirit with me strengthening,/ For ever and for evermore. Amen.'

Orange Juice

Jacob woke up suddenly and thought, 'The Lord is in this place, and I didn't even know it.' Then Jacob became frightened and said, 'This is a fearsome place! It must be the house of God and the ladder to heaven.'

GENESIS 28:16–17

THE HOUSE

The Big Breakfast

Jacob's on the run, like many of us. He doesn't want to have to take responsibility for his actions, so he just goes AWOL. Then what happens? In the middle of nowhere, while he's asleep on a rock, Jacob dreams of heaven opening and stairs coming down and landing right next to him. What does he say? 'Oh, this desert must be God's house, and I just didn't notice.' Well, that's one way of looking at it. Jacob builds an altar and declares that this particular spot in the wilderness is the 'gate of heaven'.

According to research, about two out of every five of you reading this will have had a similarly dramatic experience of the spiritual dimension in your life. Many of you have never told anyone about it, either because you think people will laugh at you or because you think it doesn't fit in with what you ought to believe. Well, that's what happened to Jacob. He was blown away. Because he hadn't talked to anyone else about his experience, he thought that that particular place was where God lived. Nope. God lives everywhere, but we can all experience him *as if* he lives right here in our living rooms.

Continental

After the philosopher Blaise Pascal had died, a paper dated 23 November 1654 was found in the lining of his coat. Here is an extract from it: 'FIRE. God of Abraham, God of Jacob, not of philosophers and scholars. Certainty. Certainty. Feeling. Joy. Peace.'

Coffee

Wherever you are, imagine that you can see what Jacob saw: a staircase leading up to heaven, with angels going up and down on it. Take a minute to hold the image. Now talk to God about how you want him to be present in your life.

Orange Juice

Since Jacob was in love with Rachel, he answered, 'If you will let me marry Rachel, I'll work seven years for you.' ... Jacob worked seven years for Laban, but the time seemed like only a few days, because he loved Rachel so much.

GENESIS 29:18-20

NOW *THAT'S* LOVE

The Big Breakfast

Jacob's mum had actually sent him to stay with her relatives, and as often happens in such stories (move over, Jane Austen), he falls in love with the boss's daughter, Rachel. Laban, Rachel's dad, has other plans. Rachel, you see, is the younger of two sisters, and Laban wants the older sister, Leah, to get married first. In a perfect daytime-TV plot twist, Laban puts Leah in a veil, shoves her into Jacob's tent in the middle of the night, and lo and behold, Jacob's married the wrong woman – after working for seven years to marry Rachel!

Probably the irony of the situation is not lost on you: the lying, cheating Jacob *does* ultimately get back what he paid out to his brother. Still, Jacob is redeemed by his love for Rachel: he stays around another seven years in order to marry her too. Would you wait fourteen years for the one you loved?

Continental

'Where there is no love there is no sense either' (Fyodor Dostoevsky).

Coffee

Is there someone who needs you to tell them today that you love them?

Orange Juice
Then Jacob, his wives, and his children got on camels and left for the home of his father Isaac in Canaan. Jacob took all the flocks, herds, and other property that he had got in northern Syria.

GENESIS 31:17-18

FACING UP TO THE PAST

The Big Breakfast
How long does it take someone to admit their wrongs and atone for them? How long is a piece of string? For Jacob, it took many, many years. That's not unusual. Families stay broken for life after one single argument because nobody wants to admit that they were at fault. It's hard. You're afraid of being vulnerable because the other person might take advantage of you. Well, that's true. Tough luck. We have Jesus for a role model.

In the year 2000 the Pope apologized for many of the sins of the Catholic Church over the years. It takes a lot of courage to do something like that. Part of you thinks, 'Surely it's best to just forget about it and hope everyone else does.' But we all know which voice that is. The person who has been wronged carries their pain round with them, and the easiest way for them to let go is for you to say sorry.

In David Lynch's book *The Straight Story*, one old man travels across the Eastern USA on a motorized lawnmower to be reconciled to his brother. It's a true story, just like our story here, and it's both ordinary and extraordinary at the same time. That's life.

Continental
'Whoever says, "I will sin and repent, and again sin and repent", will be denied the power of repenting' (Jomah 8:9, from the *Mishnah*, a collection of Jewish religious writings).

Coffee
Talk to God about any business you might have in this department, and receive his freeing forgiveness.

Orange Juice

When the messengers returned, they told Jacob, 'We went to your brother Esau, and now he is heading this way with four hundred men.'

GENESIS 32:6

SECOND THOUGHTS

The Big Breakfast

So Jacob goes back to find his brother, sending all kinds of stuff on ahead of him as presents and messengers to give him some impression of how his brother is going to react. Can you imagine what Jacob feels when he hears the news above? What would you have done? Fortunately Jacob isn't you or me, and he prays, reminding God (or is it himself?) that he had said he would look after Jacob. So he sends on his whole entourage ahead of him and offers them (wives, children and all) to his older brother as a peace offering.

Fear can make us do really stupid things sometimes. The Bible tells us that 'perfect love casts out all fear', but sometimes that feels 'easier said than done'. I like what Paul says to Timothy: 'God 's Spirit doesn't make cowards out of us. The Spirit gives us power, love, and self-control' (2 Timothy 1:7). We love the first two and try to ignore the last, but in this case that seems to be what Jacob summoned up from deep within: the self-control to do the right thing, even though he was terrified.

And, of course, what we find (later on in the story) is that Esau has done the godly thing and forgiven his brother ages ago. Shame on you, Jacob!

Continental

'Forgiveness is the answer to the child's dream of a miracle by which what is broken is made whole again, what is soiled is again made clean' (Dag Hammarskjold).

Coffee

If you are going to overcome fear in your life, which could you do with right now: love, power or self-control?

Orange Juice
… a man wrestled with him till daybreak … Then the man said, 'Let me go, for it is daybreak.' But Jacob replied, 'I will not let you go until you bless me.'

GENESIS 32:24–26 NIV

A NIGHT TO REMEMBER

The Big Breakfast
Before Jacob actually met his brother, he spent a night on his own in the wilderness. Sounds familiar, huh? There are many recurring themes in this story, and Jacob's secret meetings with God are just one of them. This time there's no staircase, but instead a night-long wrestling match with – who?

One thing about this story is that Jacob is still his usual self: gimme, gimme, gimme. 'I won't let go until you bless me.' Typical Jacob. Yet, of course, Jacob gets his way. But what does this mean? If we are selfish for long enough everyone, even God, will give in to us? I hope not. I *think* what the story has to teach us is that even the nasty bits of us can be transformed into good bits.

Sometimes I'm not too sure about the whole 'Imitation of Christ' school of thought. Does it mean that we all have to grow beards and wear white dresses? Hopefully it means we should aim to be ourselves in God, which for Jacob meant ceasing to bother other people for stuff and starting to bother God for stuff – commonly called praying.

Continental
God is waiting for you to ask him for the things he wants to give you …

Coffee
How would you like God to bless you?

Orange Juice

'Look what you've done! Now I'm in real trouble with the Canaanites and Perizzites who live around here …' They answered, 'Was it right to let our own sister be treated that way?'

GENESIS 34:30–31

HOME SWEET HOME

The Big Breakfast

Jacob and his family have arrived home, and what happens? Disaster, of course. One of Jacob's daughters is raped by the son of a local ruler, and while Jacob is trying to arrange a shotgun wedding in order to keep the peace, two of his sons take matters into their own hands and slaughter the entire village where the rapist and his father live. It's hard to know whose side to be on: the brothers, who have just killed a whole community of innocents because of the crime of one man; or Jacob, who is more concerned with his position in society than justice for his daughter. Ho hum.

This kind of story is not uncommon in the Bible. There is rape, murder and intrigue all over the place, so it's always amusing to me when people say things like, 'Oh, the Bible is so irrelevant to modern life' or 'Everyone in the Bible is goody-goody, so I can't possibly relate to them.' Ha ha HA!

It seems to me that sometimes Christians read the Bible expecting people like Jacob to be perfect and that we should be able to just read off the page how God-followers should behave. Yet the Bible is an accurate recording of what it's like to *try* to follow God, and most of us reading this know that we all fail quite a lot. Thank God that he sent Jesus to save us!

Continental

Simeon and Levi killed to avenge their sister's rape. Does that make them good brothers?

Coffee

If you found yourself in a position similar to that of the brothers, how would you react? Is that different from how God might want you to react?

Orange Juice

'We'll go to Bethel. I will build an altar there for God, who answered my prayers when I was in trouble and who has always been at my side.'

GENESIS 35:3

PRACTICAL HOLINESS

The Big Breakfast

So what do you do? Your sons have just blown it, and for all you know, there could be an army on its way right now to wipe out your entire family, God's promises or not. Jacob listens to God, who tells him that his real home is Bethel, the place where Jacob first met God in a powerful way. Maybe Jacob was running away, but maybe he was also realizing that his real home, however dry and dusty that might be, would always be the place where he met God.

In my church we have tried to make a big deal of being 'in the world but not of it'. Lots of people have got jobs as a way of meeting people and not just for the money. For some people this has been brilliant, and we have seen other people getting to know God through them. For others, it has not been an easy ride at all. They discover that there are lots of people seemingly having a good time out there. In order to survive, they need to find their own 'Bethel' – a place where they can meet God and call it 'home'.

Continental

God is where we belong. If any other thing is central to our lives, we will always be homeless.

Coffee

Is your 'Bethel' a real or imaginary place? Resolve to spend more time there this year.

Orange Juice
Here is my message for Israel: 'I am the LORD! And with my mighty power I will punish the Egyptians and free you from slavery …'

EXODUS 6:6

WHAT IS FREEDOM?

The Big Breakfast
In my humble opinion, only the word 'love' is more misused than the word 'freedom'. This passage probably represents our immediate understanding of freedom. Certainly, when I think of freedom, it tends to be in a declaration-of-human-rights kind of way.

God tells Moses that it is his will and plan to free the Israelites from their slavery in Egypt, and to take them to the homeland in Palestine. This is what I would call simple political freedom: the ability to get on with my life without undue coercion from other people. Obviously, the people of God had their own laws, so we're not really talking about any kind of absolute freedom, just the freedom to be the people God wanted them to be.

It's worth remembering that there are still many Christians who live in countries where such freedoms are unavailable to them. I have even met leaders from churches in Eastern Europe who are uncomfortable with their new-found freedom and try to rule their congregations in the old-style, communist way.

Continental
Sting once sang, 'If you love somebody, set them free.' That's clearly what God has done with us in giving us free will, but what does it mean for us?

Coffee
Pray for new Christians in countries where it is illegal to convert. They need our support, as many of them live in fear of imprisonment or death. Pray that you can use your own freedom wisely.

Orange Juice

As soon as she touched [his clothes], her bleeding stopped, and she knew she was well.

MARK 5:29

FREEDOM FOR THE BODY

The Big Breakfast

Reading the Bible gives us a much bigger picture of freedom. God is concerned not only about our political freedom, but also about our freedom from physical pain, disability and harm. Now, I know that a significant proportion of you reading this will have either a permanent disability or a temporary illness, even if it's only a cold. If God hasn't healed you, how can I write this stuff?

My initial answer is that I am only reasserting what's there in the Bible, and it causes me some discomfort to state something which, at first glance, can be offensive to many people. Why doesn't God heal *me*? All I can say from my own reading of the Bible and experience is that God doesn't always get his way. I realize I've just opened up a huge can of worms, so I'll stop right there.

Nonetheless, I'm convinced that God cares about our bodies as much as he cares about our souls. If we choose to see freedom in this wider sense, things already start to expand a bit. Doctors are freedom-fighters! When you are praying for a friend to be healed, this isn't just a kind act but a work of the Kingdom of God.

Continental

Christians often distinguish between evangelism and social action as if the former were the *real* good news and the latter were a second-rate substitute. Why?

Coffee

Can you pray for someone you know who is suffering physically? Maybe you can't believe that God would heal them, but perhaps you can just pray that God will bless them and be near to them.

Orange Juice

You will know the truth, and the truth will set you free.

JOHN 8:32

FREEDOM FOR THE MIND

The Big Breakfast

I've had the opportunity to visit Prague a number of times in the last few years, and of all the beautiful things in that most beautiful city, my favourite single thing is a simple inscription in the huge cathedral next to Prague Castle. It reads, 'Truth will win.' This simple statement was made by the early Protestant martyr Jan Huss, whose statue now dominates the main square of the city. What's great about the inscription is that the cathedral is Roman Catholic, and has been put there not as some perverse statement of victory, but as a sign of unity.

Truth is not nearly as 'cool' as freedom. Truth is hard and uncompromising, whereas freedom is big and cuddly and, by definition, wouldn't want to bother you with anything that might change your life. Yet Jesus is saying here that the truth will set us free. How? Well, ask someone who's trying to make a difficult decision, and they'll tell you how much the truth could set them free.

Although I still have many doubts, I am basically sure of Jesus and his message. This sets me free on so many levels: free to get on with my life without having to worry about its meaning all the time; free to make mistakes and know I'm forgiven; free to love, knowing I am loved. The list goes on.

Continental

'What is truth? Truth is something so noble that if God could turn aside from it, I could keep to the truth and let God go' (Meister Eckhart). What do you think?

Coffee

If you have doubts and questions, why not start dealing with them by talking to God about them and resolving to study until you know the truth?

Orange Juice

You used to be slaves of sin. But I thank God that with all your heart you obeyed the teaching you received from me. Now you are set free from sin and are slaves who please God.

ROMANS 6:17–18

FREEDOM FOR THE SOUL

The Big Breakfast

Through my church work I know lots of young people who are exploring the world and trying to work out who they are and how they should live. What they want more than anything else is the freedom to do this. What they don't want is me or anyone else telling them how they should live.

I think I could cope with this, if it wasn't for the obvious fact that they are not free at all. Here are some real quotes: 'I can't help going out with him.' 'Everybody else is doing it, so you can't expect me to be different.' 'It just comes naturally.' 'It's who I am, so how can it be wrong?'

To me all these people are slaves – slaves to sin and to what the Bible calls 'the flesh' – the desires that do sometimes seem to rule us. The kind of freedom that Paul is talking about here is extremely unfashionable in today's world, because somehow we've got the message that the only way to be happy is to indulge every desire we have to the max. Unfortunately, what this has created in our society is a whole class of thrill addicts, who need to take more drugs, have more sex, get more drunk as, each time, the thrill decreases. We're not made to live this way. God wants us to be free to rule over our nature, not to be ruled by it. In this way we become 'slaves to righteousness'.

Continental

'Sin is a small word with "I" in the middle.' In today's world of 'greed is good' and 'every man for himself', how can you break the mould and live for God and others?

Coffee

Spend some time bringing your own struggles with sin to God. Focus on his forgiveness, and ask him to fill you with his Holy Spirit so you can live for him.

Orange Juice

Christ has set us free! This means we are really free. Now hold on to your freedom and don't ever become slaves of the Law again.

GALATIANS 5:1

GOD LOVES FREEDOM!

The Big Breakfast

Here we go again! This is Paul again, who wrote yesterday's passage, only this time he's saying that we *shouldn't* be slaves. How confusing!

But this is the problem with taking bits of the Bible and looking at them on their own. If you look at the whole of Galatians you'll read about the amazing time when the early Christians decided to accept non-Jews into the Church. But this wasn't accepted by everybody. Galatians was written by Paul to a church that was at war with itself over whether non-Jews had to be circumcised to become members. Paul is saying that in Jesus we are not only free from our own selfishness, but we must also remain free from religion.

Preachers don't often say, 'Don't do what I tell you, just listen to God and read the Bible for yourself. Whatever you do, don't conform to this church's idea of what is acceptable!' To be fair, that was one of the key messages of the Reformation, but somehow things didn't change all that much. In the words of the seventies group The Who, 'Here comes the new boss, same as the old boss.' At least we have a manifesto for religious freedom here in the Bible.

Continental

Christianity is about freedom in all respects except one: we are slaves of him who made us, loves us, saved us and leads us.

Coffee

The freedom that God gives us is like the freedom given to the prodigal son and his brother (see Luke 15:11–32). We can take everything from God and blow it, or we can be faithful to God without realizing what God has given us. Think about how you would have dealt with all that freedom. Talk to God about it.

Orange Juice
The Lord God said, 'It isn't good for the man to live alone ...'

GENESIS 2:18

WHAT'S THE POINT OF CHURCH?

The Big Breakfast
There's an ancient story from the East that goes like this: the first man gets lonely, and asks God for a friend, so God creates woman. Man thinks this is great, and for a while man and woman get along just fine. Then things start to niggle, and eventually man and woman have such a fall-out that man goes back to God and says, 'Please can you take woman away. I don't like her after all.' So God takes woman away and leaves man to his devices. Then, guess what? Yep, that's right – after a while man returns to God and asks if he can have woman back ...

Men and women not only can't make up their minds about each other, but we're all caught up in this strange love-hate thing with each other. It doesn't take a brain surgeon to tell me that being a Christian on my own is hard. If you are someone who's trying to follow Jesus but is not exactly keen to go to church, you are part of an illustrious crowd which includes many well-known Christians and lots of not-so-well-known ones, like me (sometimes). It's just that the truth is that I'm even worse off on my own. We're just meant to be together, and the Church of Jesus should be the place where we discover what community is really meant to be about.

Continental
'Don't stay away from church because there are so many hypocrites. There's always room for one more' (A. R. Adams).

Coffee
Lots of people complain about what the Church is or isn't doing. Remembering that as a Christian you are as much a part of the Church as any other Christian – what are you doing?

Orange Juice
They devoted themselves to the apostles' teaching and to the fellowship, to the breaking of bread and to prayer.

ACTS 2:42 NIV

DOING THE BUSINESS

The Big Breakfast
What's the point of church? Well, I don't think it's to do with any of the things mentioned in this passage. I think it's to obey the commands that Jesus gave us when he left us (Matthew 28:18–20; see p. 123).

The truth is that when the disciples – now called apostles – thought about how they were going to make disciples, church is what happened. Our job is to bring people into the Kingdom of God, and church is the best way of doing it. Jesus only mentioned church twice: once to institute Peter as its leader, and once to give advice on how to sort out problems. He wasn't that bothered with church in itself, but he *was* bothered with teaching people to obey his commands.

Church is about enabling you and your Christian friends to do God's business in the world more effectively. Sometimes church becomes a self-feeding institution, but that doesn't mean it's a bad idea. Find me a Christian who can do without teaching, fellowship, communion and prayer, and I'll eat my Bible. These things are meant to be done together, so that we can get on with the rest of our lives in the power of the Holy Spirit.

Continental
'The church is the only co-operative society which exists for the benefit of its non-members' (Archbishop Temple).

Coffee
Think about the most important places where you receive teaching, fellowship, communion/worship and prayer. How can you improve these meetings/relationships for the benefit of others and yourself?

Orange Juice

Some people have got out of the habit of meeting for worship, but we must not do that. We should keep on encouraging each other, especially since you know that the day of the Lord's coming is getting closer. **HEBREWS 10:25**

THE BIBLE'S QUITTERS

The Big Breakfast

You may not believe it, but the Bible has the habit of telling us to do something and then admitting that no one's ever achieved it before. Here, right after all those great letters from Paul about how church should be, we have a letter to a church that's failing and falling apart. Seems silly, doesn't it? If you want to convince us that we can do this church thing, why admit that the people who started it didn't succeed?

But that's the great thing about the Bible: it pulls absolutely no punches. There's no way of reading the letter to the Hebrews (we're not sure who wrote it) except as a big kick up the behind to a church on the verge of giving up. Some of the Christians for whom this letter was written had obviously already stopped going to church. Probably the local DIY store had started opening on a Sunday and there was a great Christians versus Lions match on the TV that afternoon. Probably there were the usual serious conflicts that overtake churches from time to time: 'He sat in my seat!' 'She forgot to make the tea!' and so on. It's all so *normal*.

Continental

I once had the pleasure of chatting to one of Britain's major church leaders. We were talking about how church was really boring, and he suddenly said, 'I don't know what the problem is with "boring". Lots of things in life are boring, but we just get on with them.' What do you think?

Coffee

If you are a church member, why not do something extra for the good of others rather than yourself? If you don't go to church, how about giving it a try? (If you used to go, how about trying it again?) Talk to God about what you're going to do.

Orange Juice

First, God chose some people to be apostles and prophets and teachers for the church. But he also chose some to perform miracles or heal the sick or help others or be leaders or speak different kinds of languages.

1 CORINTHIANS 12:28

THE KENNEDY FACTOR

The Big Breakfast

It's one of the most over-used and misused quotes ever. John F. Kennedy speaks to the American people and says, 'Ask not what your country can do for you, but what you can do for your country.' Great speech. Only they killed him. Probably not because of that speech, but certainly because he wanted to do things differently.

Imagine a similar revolution in church: people coming together as a community wanting to serve each other and bring their gifts for the enhancement of others' lives. No more, 'What *do* we pay the minister for?' No more, 'I got absolutely nothing from that worship time.' No more, 'I just come to receive, I don't feel called to give anything right now.'

Well, the interesting news is that this seems to be pretty much God's plan. OK, so maybe you might feel (like me) a little intimidated with being an apostle, a prophet or a worker of miracles, but try getting out of being a teacher, a helper, an administrator. If you look through the Bible you'll find there are gifts of making things, of being friendly, of lots of things that we all do. That means, of course, that we have the same responsibility to put our tuppence-worth into the pot as everyone else.

Continental

'No one can have God for a Father who refuses to have the church for a mother' (St Augustine).

Coffee

Is there something you could give to your church? It could be a specific gift, or time, or money, or a commitment to pray. Take a minute to think of something that you have, or can do, that would help your church.

Orange Juice

The body of Christ has many different parts, just as any other body does ... But God's Spirit baptized each of us and made us part of the body of Christ. Now we each drink from that same Spirit. *1 CORINTHIANS 12:12–13*

A BIOLOGY LESSON

The Big Breakfast

When we're conceived, we start life as one cell. Inside that cell is all the information that tells all future cells what each one is going to be (the DNA). So, one cell finds out that it's going to be a liver cell, while another finds out that it's going to be a skin cell, and so on.

As Christians we're all cells in the body of Christ; we just get given different roles in the body. Yet each cell has all the information needed for every cell in the body. Even if we feel like the corn on the left big toe of the body of Jesus, we have within us the Holy Spirit – God – so that from us a whole body can grow.

Apart from in *The Addams Family*, I've never actually seen a hand alive on its own. That's a fairly important body principle. No matter how wonderful a person you are, you are never going to survive on your own. We live off each other, and there's no point denying it. Just find another member of the body (an individual or a church) who can transmit God's life to you, and hold on for dear life – I mean that literally!

Continental

'The church is one body – you cannot touch a toe without affecting the whole body' (Friedrich Tholuck).

Coffee

How can you improve your connectedness to the rest of the body? Listen to God today and see if there is something particular you can do.

Orange Juice
Peter then got out of the boat and started walking on the water towards him. But when Peter saw how strong the wind was, he was afraid and started sinking. 'Save me, Lord!' he shouted. **MATTHEW 14:29-30**

DEALING WITH DOUBT

The Big Breakfast
Peter, the guy who ended up as one of the major founders of the church, is found here *not* walking on water. He is just like us, spectacularly achieving the miraculous and then spectacularly messing up. He had it, but he lost it. Sound familiar? Sometimes I read about great heroes of the Christian faith and I feel terrible. I believe all those bits where they do amazing things, but where they admit to doubts, I seem to brush over them, thinking to myself, 'Oh, but they don't have doubts like *I* do.' Which is, of course, rubbish. You can't put your trust in God unless there is a chance he might fail you – otherwise it wouldn't be trust. You can't have faith without doubt.

A psychologist once surveyed the congregation of a large, successful church. It was the kind of church where God seemed to be doing amazing things and all the people had their lives sorted out. However, in the privacy of a questionnaire, over 80% admitted to serious doubts. For the vast majority of these people, no one else in the church knew about their struggles, because as they looked out at this wonderful, successful congregation, they imagined that they must be the only one among thousands who didn't get it. You can't help thinking, 'If only…'

Continental
'Faith which does not doubt is dead faith' (Miguel de Unamuno).

Coffee
Telling yourself and God the truth can be a hard experience, but you cannot deal with your doubts until you face them head on. Sometimes writing God a letter allows you a comfortable way of expressing things that don't come easily.

Orange Juice

Be merciful to those who doubt …

JUDE 22 NIV

AND THE PUNISHMENT FOR DOUBT IS ...

The Big Breakfast

People don't read the book of Jude too often. It's so small that it doesn't seem worthy of consideration. But here's a little gem that lots of Christians need to check out, because, let's face it, our response to Christians who doubt is often less than merciful.

There are a number of common responses: 'Oh no, you can't doubt that, because the Bible says it's true.' 'Oh no, that means that you're going to lose your faith and leave the church.' 'Oh no, this is happening because there's sin in your life.'

Sometimes these statements can be true, but the point is that when people own up to doubt, they don't get mercy, they get 'Oh no.' This makes it really, really hard to own up to what's actually going on inside us, so that we can end up feeling out on the edge of faith without even wanting to. A friend of mine who is struggling with her faith came to see me with all kinds of weird books that a guy had given her, and I suddenly realized that if I wasn't going to help her work through her outlook on life, there are plenty of others who will.

Continental

'There lives more faith in honest doubt,/ Believe me, than in half the creeds' (Alfred, Lord Tennyson).

Coffee

Think about how you may have reacted in the past to a fellow Christian who you felt had 'let you down'. If you were not merciful, repent and resolve to be more like Jesus in dealing with doubt in the future.

Orange Juice

Straight away the boy's father shouted, 'I do have faith! Please help me to have even more.'

MARK 9:24

SWIMMING AGAINST THE STREAM

The Big Breakfast

You probably remember this story: Jesus has been approached by the father of a boy who – to our eyes, at least – seems to be epileptic. The cause is a demon, and the father is hoping that Jesus will sort out the boy. 'Anything is possible for someone who has faith!' says Jesus in verse 23, and verse 24 shows how the father responds.

I completely identify with what he's saying. Ask me if I believe that God can heal an epileptic and/or cast out a demon, my response would always be 'Yes, absolutely.' Yet when it comes to praying for people who are ill, my 'faith' suddenly feels very weak indeed.

Yet the faith of this father, such as it was, was enough. On another occasion Jesus said we only need faith the size of a mustard seed, which is great! Later the disciples talked to Jesus, admitting that they hadn't been able to heal the boy. He explained that this kind of demon only came out by prayer, which seems to me to indicate faith in the wrong thing: these guys had probably just declared healing over the boy, without remembering who it was that was doing the healing. The best kind of faith always comes by prayer: Jesus said he only ever did what he saw his Father doing.

Continental

'Either God exists or he does not. But to which side shall we lean? … A game is being played, at the extremity of this infinite distance, where heads or tails will fall. What will you bet? … If you win, you win everything; if you lose, you lose nothing. Bet then that he exists, without hesitating' (Blaise Pascal).

Coffee

If you find it hard to believe in God, spend the day as if you do. If you find it easy to believe in God, spend the day as if you didn't. Either way, you will hopefully learn something new about yourself, others and the world around you.

Orange Juice

Jesus ... said to Thomas, 'Put your finger here and look at my hands! Put your hand into my side. Stop doubting and have faith!'

JOHN 20:26-27

THE POWER OF TOUCH

The Big Breakfast

It's not fair, is it? There are only a few people who have had the privilege of having their doubts completely blown out of the water by meeting the living God. The echo of that encounter with the risen Jesus is what powers the church to this day: those guys really saw him! And that started the biggest movement the human race has ever seen.

I have quite a few friends who became what I call 'semi-retired Christians' in their twenties. It was too hard to believe, or too hard to do, so they just 'toned down' all the difficult bits. Today many of them seem nostalgic for a time when they once had a reason to live.

Without the chance of putting a hand in Jesus' side, it's hard to say to such people, 'Stop doubting and believe,' but I think there are times when that is the right response. Doubt can make your life turn to ice, freezing every decision and every way forward. Sometimes you need to jump out in faith and step onto what looks like thin ice ... then you'll know if your doubts are well founded. If God is real, he can cope with the odd challenge!

Continental

'Faith is the daring of the soul to go farther than it can see' (William Clarke).

Coffee

Spend a little bit of time in quiet, thinking about big decisions you have to make and/or scary things you have to do. Can you agree with God to take a leap of faith? What would that mean for you in the situation you are thinking of?

Orange Juice

Jesus heard what they said, and he said to Jairus, 'Don't worry. Just have faith!'

MARK 5:36

WISE WORDS TO A WISE MAN

The Big Breakfast

This particular synagogue leader, Jairus, had a daughter who was sick, and Jesus did his belief bit – so frustrating! I just wish he would say, 'It's OK, it's nothing to do with you, I'll heal your daughter.' He doesn't, and that seems to be the deal throughout the Bible: God and humanity in partnership.

I don't know how often you look back on your day and try to see what God was doing in it, but I recommend that you try it every now and again. If you spend the day looking out of your office window waiting for God to reveal himself in the sky, you're looking in the wrong place.

Aye, there's the rub, as someone very old once said: just at the moment when we feel like giving up, we need to carry on living in faith. Being a Christian is a bit like seeing the world through God's glasses: we are always free to take them off, and when we do, of course the world looks different. The funny thing about removing those glasses, though, is that the world makes even less sense! Being a Christian can be scary, because we're giving up all our self-determination to someone we can't even see. But it's something that can't be done in half-measure.

Continental

'Christianity hasn't been tried and found wanting, it's been found difficult and left untried' (G. K. Chesterton).

Coffee

What do you need to do to deal with your questions? Talk to God and listen to see if he has anything to say. Then decide what your first step is and *just do it*!

Orange Juice

When the builders had finished laying the foundations of the temple, the priests put on their robes and blew trumpets in honour of the LORD … They praised the LORD and gave thanks … singing: 'The LORD is good! His faithful love for Israel will last for ever.'

EZRA 3:10–11

FOUNDATIONS

The Big Breakfast

Ezra and Nehemiah are not the best-known books in the Bible, by a long way. However, I think these two books have a lot to say to us in the West. They describe a situation in which a small group of people faithful to God (the Jews returning from exile in Babylon) is trying to re-establish their religion in their homeland. It's not the most exciting story ever – lots of building, basically – but it is about the hard slog that many of us feel as we try to sort out being a Christian in what is often called a post-Christian environment.

Here, early on in the book of Ezra, the first few people have returned and have built the foundation of a new temple for God. Even though the temple isn't even near finished, they take the opportunity to get all their fancy gear on and praise God.

This is not always something I do – praising God when things aren't sorted out yet. God has to answer *all* my prayers before he gets any thanks from me! But reading this passage, I feel that maybe our worship today has lost something. It seems like these guys were desperate to worship God and did so at the earliest opportunity. Hmm … how often do I feel like that?

Continental

The famous Westminster Confession asks the question, 'What is the chief end of man?' The answer is: 'To glorify God and enjoy him forever.'

Coffee

Praise God! If you can't find the words, just use the phrase in today's passage – 'His faithful love for Israel will last for ever' – replacing 'Israel' with 'me' or 'us'.

Orange Juice

Many of the older priests and Levites and the heads of families cried aloud because they remembered seeing the first temple years before. But others were so happy that they celebrated with joyful shouts.

EZRA 3:12

TEARS AND LAUGHTER

The Big Breakfast

The church in the English-speaking world didn't deal very well with the 20th century at all, and as we begin to peep our heads above the parapet, we now see that things are very different from the time when the church was a vital part of our communities. What can we do? God's people began by restoring the temple worship of God, as we saw yesterday. But look at how the different people present on that day reacted: the older ones were crying, the younger ones were leaping with joy. Why was this?

Here's my suggestion: those who had seen the previous temple, destroyed 70 years earlier, knew that its destruction was a direct result of them messing up. They've spent their entire lives in exile, and only now do they understand what they've missed. The younger ones are in at the start of something exciting and new, and have the chance to become history-makers.

How easy it is for the one to become the other: all you have to do is compromise on the dreams God has given you, and you'll soon find yourself looking back on your life and wondering where it all went wrong. Don't give up.

Continental

In Nikos Kazantzakis' famous novel *The Last Temptation*, Jesus' greatest weakness isn't his desire to be powerful and famous, but his desire to be normal, to settle down and disappear into the crowd. How about you?

Coffee

What God-given dreams do you have for your life? Celebrate the fact that you have so much life ahead of you to fulfil them. You might want to write them down and put them by the side of your bed or in your Bible to remind you of what God has called you to.

Orange Juice
Then the neighbouring people began to do everything possible to frighten the Jews and to make them stop building … they kept bribing government officials to slow down the work.

EZRA 4:4–5

NOISE ATTRACTS TROUBLE

The Big Breakfast
This passage follows on immediately from yesterday's, and we get a little bit of dramatic interpretation of events: the praise of God's people is 'heard a long way off', and what happens? Yep, the enemies of Judah hear about what's going on.

Not long ago I met a man who claimed he could see demons. I was, I admit, a bit freaked by this – even more so when he explained that he generally saw most demons at Christian meetings! I avoided him after that!

Actually, this is not such a mad idea. C. S. Lewis' classic book *The Screwtape Letters* is basically about how a minor demon tempts a young Christian. It shouldn't really surprise us: why would the enemy bother with those who can't be bothered with Jesus? After all, he has them right where he wants them.

There's no escaping from the fact that building anything for God is going to attract the attention of his enemies. Even modern 'heroes' of the faith like Mother Teresa and Desmond Tutu had their detractors. Because of this, worship of God, and work for him, should never be undertaken lightly: both are an act of spiritual warfare, of provocation. Watch out!

Continental
'Progress towards the welfare of mankind is made not by the persecutors but by the persecuted … Only goodness, meeting evil and not being infected by it, conquers evil' (Leo Tolstoy).

Coffee
Jesus said we should rejoice if people pick on us because we are Christians. Bring your feelings about being a Christian 'in the marketplace' to God.

Orange Juice

'Many Israelites, including priests and Levites, are living just like the people around them ... Some Israelite men have married foreign women and have let their sons do the same thing.'

EZRA 9:1-2

WHAT IS HOLINESS?

The Big Breakfast

Some people suggest that God wanted the Israelites to live in complete separation from all the other tribes in the Near East. If that were the case, surely he would have put them on Cyprus, rather than at the ancient world's equivalent of Spaghetti Junction. God called the Israelites to be 'in the world, but not of it'.

Sometimes we can be too detached from the world; sometimes we can be too much into the world. This was definitely a time for stepping back from the world to re-establish the Jews' identity.

Today, I can see some Christians who appear to be lost in their own super-spiritual world, while others seem barely distinguishable from those around them. This story tells us that there can be a time to retreat from the world if we are in danger of losing our 'saltiness' (as Jesus described it), but we must remember that just as often God calls us to get out of our safety zone and live dangerously. Whichever of these sounds hardest to you is probably the one that you need to do!

Continental

To be holy is to be 'set apart' – not to sit on the sidelines, but set apart for God and for his service.

Coffee

Meditate on what it might mean for you to be 'in the world but not of it'.

Orange Juice

While Ezra was down on his knees in front of God's temple, praying with tears in his eyes, and confessing the sins of the people of Israel, a large number of men, women, and children gathered around him and cried bitterly.

EZRA 10:1

The Big Breakfast

When you realize that you've gone wrong somewhere along the line – like Ezra did – how do you react? When I find myself in a hole that I can't dig myself out of, I tend to go a bit mad. I want to know what to do to sort everything out. I'm not really hot-headed, and to call me a 'man of action' would probably make most of my friends die with laughter, but I just can't do nothing – I can't! Which is exactly what Ezra does. For what seems like ages.

If you've got the time, read through the story between yesterday's passage and today's. First of all, Ezra takes responsibility for the mess, even though (in this case) it's not his fault. He doesn't try to blame somebody else, and comes before God and cries. Think about when two friends fall out. Let's face it, nine times out of ten, each one blames the other. It's natural. But it's not Ezra.

After the crying and repenting, Ezra prays some more, and then we get to the passage above. Just like the noise of praise earlier in Ezra, the noise of repentance attracts attention too, this time from God's people. Again, if you've got time, keep reading, because Ezra's lonely sadness brings the whole nation together.

Continental

'Why am I discouraged? Why am I restless? I trust you! And I will praise you again because you help me, and you are my God' (Psalm 43:5).

Coffee

Is there a bad situation that you need to take 'ownership' of ? Taking responsibility in the way that Ezra did doesn't mean you have to take the blame, but it can help to bring God into a difficult predicament.

Orange Juice

In the year that King Uzziah died, I had a vision of the Lord. He was on his throne high above … Flaming creatures with six wings each … shouted, 'Holy, holy, holy, LORD All-Powerful! The earth is filled with your glory.'

ISAIAH 6:1–3

SLACK-JAWED

The Big Breakfast

Slack-jawed: I can't think of any other way to describe some of the amazing experiences that are recorded in the Bible. I realize that most of you reading this will never have seen a seraph (that includes me, by the way), so don't worry too much about feeling somehow inadequate in the face of the revelation in today's passage. Some of Isaiah's other visions are a bit more normal – if normal's the right word.

Think about a slack-jaw moment in your life: maybe standing on top of a mountain, watching a movie, even a brilliant sporting achievement. Allow yourself to go back to that time and remember not only the event but the feeling as well, the way the awe created physical sensations in your body.

Hold that feeling, and imagine you are in the temple in Jerusalem. You are suddenly aware that God is there, in the form of a huge man wearing a robe, which seems to go on for ever, filling the entire building. Angels (that's the seraphs) are flying around singing praises to God. What would you do? (Answer coming tomorrow …)

Continental

'The greatest need of the moment is that lighthearted, superficial religionists be struck down with a vision of God high and lifted up, with his train filling the temple' (A. W. Tozer).

Coffee

Remember that moment when you really experienced awe. Hold it for a moment and then transfer the feeling onto the image of God in today's passage. What will you say to your God?

Orange Juice
… I was seeing the brightness of the LORD's glory! So I bowed with my face to the ground, and just then I heard a voice speaking to me. The LORD said, 'Ezekiel, son of man, I want you to stand up and listen.' **EZEKIEL 1:28–2:1**

DON'T GET DOWN, GET UP!

The Big Breakfast
The first prayer meeting I remember going to as a new Christian was at the home of a friend from school. There were about ten of us and, obviously, I didn't really know what to do. Still, I learned soon enough that one of the most important things about prayer is position. Even if I never actually said a word, I could show everyone else that I was praying by leaning forward in my chair and looking at the floor.

Perhaps this shows that I only partly understood how big God is. If I had really met the Big G, I would no doubt have ended up on the floor, just as Ezekiel did. He saw God in a similarly scary fashion to Isaiah, and did what most of us would do: since you can't run away from a God who is everywhere, at least you can bury your face in the ground and hope for the best…

And then God says, 'Get up! I want you to stand before me, you've got nothing to hide!' God's like that: along with the justice comes mercy; along with the immenseness of the Creator of the universe comes the voice of a friend.

Continental
'Leonard Thynn leaned across and whispered in my ear, "He knows a different God to the one I do. His God's nice"' (*The Sacred Diary of Adrian Plass*).

Coffee
Why not try praying in a different position to the one you normally use? Even if you are sitting on a bus right now, you could always stand up, or just cup your hands as a sign of openness to God. It can make a difference!

Orange Juice

Samuel got up and opened the doors to the LORD's house. He was afraid to tell Eli what the LORD had said. But Eli told him, 'Samuel, my boy, come here!' 'Here I am,' Samuel answered.

1 SAMUEL 3:15–16

SOMETHING TO SAY?

The Big Breakfast

When I was a young Christian a preacher came to my church, and when he had finished speaking he said, 'I believe that God has something extra to say to us, and he is going to use someone in the congregation to say it.' Immediately my heart started pounding and I felt that I had something to say, but I was terrified. So I just sat there in my reverent position, trying not to catch his eye.

At the end of the service I summoned up the courage to approach the preacher and tell him what was still going round my head. 'You have sinned,' he said, 'because that was the word God wanted to bring to the church, and you have refused to give it.' Needless to say, I was devastated, and it's something I still remember to this day. You see, the thing is, I think he might have been right.

Eli was wise enough to know that God had spoken to Samuel (try reading the whole chapter for the full story). Eli wanted the truth, even though it turned out to be condemnation for him and his family. What God spoke to Samuel, he *had* to share – no choice, no get-out clause. When God tells us something, very often it's for others too.

Continental

'I wish the Lord would give his Spirit to all his people so everyone could be a prophet' (Numbers 11:29).

Coffee

Is there something that you need to tell someone else, but you don't know how? Talk to God about it, and see if there is anyone who could help you sort out whether it's God talking or not.

Orange Juice

While Peter was still thinking about the vision, the Holy Spirit said to him, 'Three men are here looking for you. Hurry down and go with them. Don't worry, I sent them.'

ACTS 10:19–20

JUST DO IT

The Big Breakfast

You can find this story in more detail on page 99. Peter had a vision and it made little sense to him until much later. Sometimes hearing from God can be like that. We may read something in the Bible and only much later do we really understand it. Or we may experience something in life and it's only looking back on it, now, that we begin to see what it was all about. That's normal. It's OK. We don't always understand everything straight away, especially when it comes to God.

Just think: one day, many hundreds of years from now, we may understand every mystery of the universe, and we will rightly feel proud of ourselves. But all we will have done is to understand something that God has made! It's like thinking we've understood humans because we've understood the wheel. God will take us a little longer – the technical term being 'eternity'.

So don't worry if God sometimes leaves you a bit befuddled – that's just what happens when the finite and the infinite meet. And it's also why Jesus came: to give us the best chance of understanding what we really need to know.

Continental

Gandhi – a great admirer of Jesus – once said that if he found just one person living out the Christian life as described by Jesus, he would become a Christian. Ouch!

Coffee

Was there a time in your life in which you can see that God was at work, even though it was hard to go through it? If so, thank God today. If not, spend a minute or two thinking about your life, and see if God shows you anything about it.

Orange Juice
I saw a large crowd with more people than could be counted ... They wore white robes and held palm branches in their hands, as they shouted, 'Our God, who sits upon the throne, has the power to save his people...

REVELATION 7:9-10

JESUS COME ON!

The Big Breakfast
There's this guy I know called Caleb who, whenever I meet him or hear of him, is always shouting, 'Come on!' He has a specially designed T-shirt which proclaims, 'Freedom come on!' But his favourite 'come on' is 'Jesus come on!' You can't really argue with that – it's how the Bible ends, in the last few verses of Revelation, only most translations put it more politely: 'Come, Lord Jesus.' But since I met Caleb, I prefer his version.

I can't wait to see what John saw: I guess it's what most of us hope for. All kinds of people – all races, nations, classes, you name it – worshipping God together. I realize that to some this will sound like hell: all those people who are *not like me* in heaven, everyone equal. But those people, if they make it, will have to enjoy it or try the other place.

Maybe that's the devil's strategy ... get us all to hate each other now so we won't be able to enjoy heaven when we get there? But he's gonna lose. We're going to meet Jesus face to face and look into his eyes and finally know what love is. I can't wait for the party. Jesus come on!

Continental
We should give God the same place in our hearts that he holds in the universe.

Coffee
Remember all that Jesus has done for you – you might want to write things down – and thank him, in whatever way seems right.

Orange Juice

'No one knows the day or hour. The angels in heaven don't know, and the Son himself doesn't know. Only the Father knows. When the Son of Man appears, things will be just as they were when Noah lived.'

MATTHEW 24:36-37

HOLD ON A MINUTE!

The Big Breakfast

Five days on the end of the world? Sounds exciting, huh? Well, maybe you've never given it much thought: the churches today aren't really full of hell-fire-and-damnation preachers like they used to be. However, the end of the world is a whole subject of study (called 'eschatology' – they have to come up with a weird name, don't they?), so maybe it's worth your while to dig a bit deeper into it than you have done previously. I'm not promising that five Bible readings are going to tell you everything you need to know: in fact, they'll probably just show you how much you don't know yet! However, let's have a go.

Continuing on the theme of not knowing everything, here's a statement from Jesus which must always be in our minds when we start getting into thinking about when God winds up the world as we know it. Jesus once said that when he returned (an important part of God's plans for the end of the universe), it would be as unexpected as when a thief breaks into your home in the middle of the night.

Lots of Christians from around the world spend huge amounts of time, money and energy trying to work out when Jesus is coming back, despite the fact that Jesus himself said we'll never know. It may be that we'll die before Jesus returns, or it may be that today's the day …

Continental

'Limited by mortality, yet destined for liberation, in hope the universe waits: God's purpose shall be revealed' (The Iona Community).

Coffee

If you knew that the world was going to end in a week and that you would then meet Jesus face to face, what would you do during that week?

Orange Juice

'Wonderful!' his master replied. 'You are a good and faithful servant. I left you in charge of only a little, but now I will put you in charge of much more. Come and share in my happiness!'

MATTHEW 25:23

TOMORROW IS THE NEXT TODAY

The Big Breakfast

You may know this story: a rich boss goes away for a while and hands out his resources to three of his most trusted workers to use as they see fit for the good of their employer. One of them buries the money – a talent (a unit of weight and currency, worth about £1,000 in today's money) – and is sent away into 'outer darkness'. But the other two invest their talents and come back to their returning boss with the interest. He is over-the-top happy: seemingly not because he's made money, but more because the two have been 'faithful' with what he has given them.

Continental

'God has not called me to be successful, he has called me to be faithful' (Mother Teresa of Calcutta).

This story is undoubtedly a picture of what it's going to be like when we meet God. He's going to say to us, 'Well, I put you in the 21st century, one of the most affluent periods in world history, with world-wide communication and travel, and I gave you the gospel to share with people and my Spirit to help you. How did you do?' How are we going to answer? 'Well, Lord, I thought your good news was so special that I buried it in the church and kept it safe.' Uh-uh.

This is one of a number of stories in the Bible that tell us that the end of the world is going to involve us meeting God and telling him what we've done with our life. So how do you feel about that?

Coffee

What 'talents' has God given you? Take a moment to thank him for all the good things in your life, and think about how you can use all you have for God.

Orange Juice
These bodies will die, but the bodies that are raised will live for ever. These ugly and weak bodies will become beautiful and strong …

1 CORINTHIANS 15:42–44

HE LOVES YOUR BODY!

The Big Breakfast
What does God think about you? Does he like you? Does he like your body? Hmmm. What do you think? Well, despite what most people seem to think about life in God's new world, we will have bodies. OK, so our bodies won't be exactly the same, but we will still be em-bodied. This is really important: we are not just spirits living in bodies short-term. God sees us as whole people and is not just concerned with the invisible bits of us.

I have a friend who hates her body. I know she's not the only one: there are millions of people in the West who suffer greatly with problems to do with their self-image. The devil tells them that their bodies are ugly because they don't look like Kate Moss/Lara Croft/insert your own ridiculous role model here. God's love of our bodies provides us with a challenge: we must fight the voices that say bodies are only beautiful if they look a certain way.

Yet there is good news for the person who feels that their body lets them down: we get a new one! What will it be like? Well, perhaps the best model for that would be Jesus, who was able to do amazing things with his resurrection body, but was still identifiable as the guy everyone knew.

Continental
'What we call the beginning is often the end/ And to make an end is to make a beginning./ The end is where we start from' (T. S. Eliot).

Coffee
Tell God which parts of 'you' you would like to take with you into your new life, and which parts you would like to leave behind.

Orange Juice

Then they sang a new song, 'You are worthy to receive the scroll and open its seals, because you were killed. And with your own blood you bought for God people from every tribe, language, nation, and race …'

REVELATION 5:9

THE MOMENT

The Big Breakfast

Maybe you're feeling a bit unsure of what you're going to say when you meet God on the so-called 'Day of Judgement'. Well, I have good news for you: God has already prepared a script for you. In the book of Revelation, God shows John, the writer, a scroll that has the names of everyone who can enter into God's new world, but the scroll can only be opened by someone who is 'worthy'. John ends up in tears because no one can be found who is worthy to open the scroll which will allow people to come into their inheritance. Then the above happens.

Here, on the biggest scale possible, is the good news about Jesus: his death opens up the gate of heaven and lets us in. Without Jesus' sacrifice for us, our resurrection on the last day would be a pretty unpleasant affair. God would look at us and say, 'Well, you're not worthy to be with me forever. Is anyone willing to stand up for this person and say they're OK?' And then there would be an eternal silence.

Jesus' death was not just an historic event: it changed history FOREVER!

Continental

'Glory be to Jesus/ Who in bitter pains/ Poured for me the life-blood/ From his sacred veins' (traditional Italian hymn).

Coffee

Imagine Jesus taking you to the front of a large queue of people trying to get into an event or nightclub. The bouncers are saying to everyone, 'Your name's not down, you're not coming in.' Then, as you approach the entrance, the bouncers say, 'Who do you think you … oh, you're with Jesus. Fine, come in.' How do you feel?

Orange Juice

Then I saw New Jerusalem, that holy city, coming down from God in heaven.

REVELATION 21:2

SO WHAT'S HEAVEN LIKE?

The Big Breakfast

Well, here we are at the end of Revelation. I've skipped all the dragons and other creatures in this book because I wanted to rush to the end to tell you what God has shown us about what life in the new creation is going to be like, and the news is: it's a big city.

That's right: no sign of any people with wings and white dresses. Now I don't know about you, but if someone asked me to picture God's perfect future for creation, I wouldn't pick a city. No way. Dirty. Smelly. Crime-ridden. No trees. And so on.

There's another thing about this city, this New Jerusalem. There's no temple, no church. That's another funny thing: I'd always imagined that life with God would be like being at church all the time. I confess to worrying about getting bored singing Christian songs for ever. Funnily enough, God's idea of perfect creation seems to have more similarities with his first effort than we had imagined. We won't need a church because wherever we go, God will be with us. Beyond that, our job will be to be a good citizen of this New Jerusalem.

Continental

'Look! Look! God has moved into the neighbourhood, making his home with men and women! They're his people, he's their God ... Look! I'm making everything new!' (Revelation 21:3–5, *The Message*).

Coffee

Try to imagine this New Jerusalem. What would it be like to walk through a big city and know that God was with you wherever you went? Allow that sense of God's presence to lead you to worship him.

Orange Juice

Your sacrifices mean nothing to me. I am sick of your offerings of rams and choice cattle; I don't like the blood of bulls or lambs or goats. Who asked you to bring all this when you come to worship me? Stay out of my temple!

ISAIAH 1:11-12

THE BAD NEWS FIRST

The Big Breakfast

Welcome to Isaiah, one of the most dense, beautiful, mysterious and misused books in the Bible. From the bits you normally hear in church, you would think that Isaiah was a book about Jesus, but in fact Isaiah is about one of the most turbulent times in the history of God's people. It covers the time of the decline and fall of the great kingdom of Israel. The political situation, as Israel broke into two and ultimately destroyed itself, was as awful as it could be, but then it got worse. Isaiah deals with the coming invasion of Judah and her exile in Babylon.

And there's no polite introduction: here we are in chapter 1, and God is saying some hard stuff to his people: 'Are you sure it was me who wanted you to worship me like this? Are you convinced that all your religious ceremonies are the kind of worship that I desire? Well, I'm not. You have created a religious system that provides you with a cheap form of grace that gets you out of taking responsibility for your lives and gets you out of having to confront *me*. Yes, I hope you remember what this is all about: you humans coming to terms with me, your God. It's not about your selfish needs and wants – leave those to me – it's about the glory of the Creator and how you are going to deal with *that*.'

Continental

'Tradition is the living faith of dead people; traditionalism is the dead faith of living people'
(Anonymous).

Coffee

Are we seeking God or seeking to salve our consciences? Ask God to show you anything in your own life that has become a way of showing yourself and others that you are 'OK', and not real worship.

Orange Juice
Stop doing wrong and learn to live right. See that justice is done ... I, the LORD, invite you to come and talk it over. Your sins are scarlet red, but they will be whiter than snow or wool.

ISAIAH 1:16–18

THE EVEN WORSE NEWS NEXT

The Big Breakfast
I'm not sure that I understand what 'love' is, to tell you the truth. Take being a parent, for example. Little Jimmy is about to put his hand in the fire: do you stop him, or do you say to yourself, 'Well, if I love him, I've got to let him go his own way ...' What a stupid question!

Unless, of course, little Jimmy is 15 and the fire is marijuana. Then suddenly (or so we're told), love is all about letting people screw up their lives and not getting involved.

Well, call me old-fashioned – 'Old Fashioned!' I hear you cry – but I just don't get it. And it seems God's approach doesn't fit in with the Jerry Springer approach to life either. 'Sort it out!' God says, rather bluntly. And that's that. 'I'm God, and I know best, so shut your mouth and get on with it.'

Continental
God convicts us of sin so that we can be forgiven, not so that we can be damned.

Coffee
There's a song my church sings that goes, 'Your army is full of power/ But you said that I could fight with you/ I still don't fight for justice.' What does 'fighting for justice' mean to you in your situation? Is there something you could resolve to do right now?

Orange Juice
In the year that King Uzziah died, I had a vision of the LORD. He was on his throne high above ... Flaming creatures with six wings each ... shouted, 'Holy, holy, holy, LORD All-Powerful! The earth is filled with your glory.'

ISAIAH 6:1-3

GOD STEPS IN

The Big Breakfast
After God lays out both the problem (fake and shallow religion) and the solution ('Let's talk it over'), he then starts looking for someone to get the message out.

I don't know if you have had an experience of God like Isaiah's, but I haven't, and I would probably need a change of underwear if I ever did. I once felt God forcing me down onto the carpet, and I think I saw some fire out of the corner of my eye, and that was enough for me! Isaiah got to see God on his throne and was obviously terrified.

Not everyone gets a call like this one, but boy, it would help in those what-*am*-I-doing-believing-this-stuff? moments. As we'll see in the next reading, it's OK to feel useless in the presence of God. In fact, I suspect any other attitude is probably a bit of a mistake. The awesomeness of God tends to get played down a bit nowadays, in our new Jesus-is-my-best-friend world. Isaiah met the Creator and Sustainer of the universe!!!

Continental
'You cannot know God as your friend until you have known him as your enemy' (Martin Luther).

Coffee
Remember a time when you became aware of the bigness of God. Try to recapture how you felt at that time. If you've never had that kind of feeling, try reading Isaiah chapter 6 and entering into the story as much as you can. How would you feel?

Orange Juice

Then I cried out, 'I'm doomed! Everything I say is sinful, and so are the words of everyone around me. Yet I have seen the King, the LORD All-Powerful.'

ISAIAH 6:5

I'M NOT WORTHY!

The Big Breakfast

Isaiah represents a major leap forward in the Bible's understanding of how God deals with sin. While the early Israelites had a complex set of laws and rituals, here Isaiah's penitence is enough for him to receive forgiveness from God. Indeed, all that we've read so far has more in common with Jesus' story about the Pharisee and the tax collector (Luke 18:10–14) than with the usual idea of the nasty old Old Testament God with big beard and even bigger lightning bolts. Again we have this mad conflict: one minute we think that we've had it because God is so great and just, and then the next minute he's offering salvation. Phew! Thank you, God!

Sometimes we forget this amazing miracle about God: 'Our God, no one is like you … you freely forgive our sin and guilt. You don't stay angry for ever; you're glad to have pity and pleased to be merciful' (Micah 7:18–19).

Continental

Jesus said, 'For everyone who exalts himself will be humbled, and he who humbles himself will be exalted' (Luke 18:14 NIV).

Coffee

Imagine an angel coming to you with a burning coal and offering to touch anything that is 'unclean' in the sight of God. Well, will you let the angel take away your sin, even though the purification might be painful? Even if you're not ready to have everything burnt up, talk to God about it.

Orange Juice

After this, I heard the LORD ask, 'Is there anyone I can send? Will someone go for us?'

'I'll go,' I answered. 'Send me!'

ISAIAH 6:8

MISSIONARY REQUIRED: ENQUIRE WITHIN

The Big Breakfast

OK, so Isaiah gets called. That's fine – he was Isaiah, not me. I'm just normal. I've not been called to Outer Mongolia or even Inner London. Isaiah was special: that's obvious because … well, because he did what he was told, for a start. And, he trusted God, which makes him almost unique in my experience. Me, I'd require any request from God to be signed in triplicate before I took any notice.

I'm not the world-changing type. I just want to sit in the corner reading my copy of *Esquire/Elle/Good Housekeeping/fill in your favourite here* and bother nobody. I've done it for years and I expect that this state of affairs will continue until the day when the Lord takes me from this terrible old world and into his glory.

I do hear this voice sometimes, saying, 'Whom shall I send?' But I just tell the voice to try Tony down the road: I once heard him pray out loud, so I imagine he must be the 'missionary type'.

Anyway, I'm not perfect. I know that all the people God used in the Bible were perfect, like David, Samson, Peter and all the saints – well, Jesus definitely – so God can't use me. Am I safe yet?

No, you're not, so stop trying and give in.

Continental

Nobody in the Bible, when given a job by God, ever said, 'Fine, that's easy.'

Coffee

How does God want to use you? Are there things that he has already asked you to do that you need to go back to? Make room for listening to God today.

Orange Juice
My servant will succeed! He will be given great praise and the highest honours. Many were horrified at what happened to him … My servant will make nations worthy to worship me …

ISAIAH 52:13–15

THE MAN

The Big Breakfast
We've leapt forward a bit here! The long and the short of it was that despite God's offer of reconciliation, Judah did, of course, end up being exiled. These next five readings come from the second part of Isaiah, which is looking further ahead to a time when God will return his people to Jerusalem (see the readings on Ezra and Nehemiah for that story).

'When Isaiah wrote about God's servant, he was thinking primarily about the terrible state that God's people were in and how their faithfulness would eventually be vindicated. Little did he know that his immediate prophetic insight into the affairs of Israel would take on such significance when Jesus appeared on the scene! There's a lot of that kind of prophecy in the Bible: there is an immediate meaning and a kind of subtext, a God-given bigger picture.

It's good to be reminded of this truth: while God is looking right at us, he's still aware of what's going on around the universe, and vice versa. In an age where we're expected to work, look after our family, have a beautiful body, go on holiday *and* be holy, we should remember that God is the original multi-tasker.

Continental
In this upwardly-mobile world, are you prepared to follow God's wise servant and maybe even be downwardly mobile?

Coffee
Is there someone you know who is often seen as an outsider or a reject? Pray for that person; maybe you could try to spend some time with them.

Orange Juice

If you are thirsty, come and drink water! If you don't have any money, come, eat what you want! Drink wine and milk without paying a penny.

ISAIAH 55:1

A *VERY* SPECIAL OFFER

The Big Breakfast

Marx had a point: he described religion (he was talking mainly about Christianity) as 'the opium of the masses', because poor people who should have been more angry about their lot were kept happy by faith.

It's a toughie, because over the years rich Christians *have* told poor Christians not to moan about being poor and just to carry on being happy and paying their taxes. The Favourite English Hymn, 'All Things Bright and Beautiful', contains a verse which goes, 'The rich man in his castle,/ The poor man at his gate,/ God made them rich and poor …' Well, you get the idea. However, Christians all over the world have fought for political, social and economic freedom for themselves and their brothers and sisters.

This beautiful passage challenges God's people to change their attitude towards material possessions. But we know, even from elsewhere in Isaiah, that God cares about everyone having enough to eat and drink. God's not telling us to go live in a shed in the woods and eat nuts and berries, but he is reminding us that all that stuff we work for is, in ultimate terms, pretty useless.

Continental

'But put God's work first, and these things will be yours as well' (Luke 12:32).

Coffee

Just read the passage to yourself a couple of times, picking out a phrase or two to really think on. Meditate on the words and let God speak to you.

Orange Juice

The Spirit of the Sovereign LORD is on me, because the LORD has anointed me to preach good news to the poor. He has sent me to bind up the broken-hearted, to proclaim freedom for the captives and release for the prisoners…

ISAIAH 61:1 NIV

THE JESUS MANIFESTO

The Big Breakfast

I love this passage. I have a really vivid image in my head of that moment in Luke chapter 4 where Jesus reads it out, and as the villagers sit in silence waiting for Jesus to comment on the meaning of the text, he says simply, 'What you have just heard me read has come true today' (verse 21). Drama! It's another of these passages which had a special meaning at the exact time when it was written as well as the meaning given to it by Jesus. One of the special things about this passage is the fact that, in the middle of all this stuff about the servant, the same person is 'anointed', something which implies a king and/or priest. So, the servant is also a king … Now, who could that be …?

A bit like an anagram on a TV quiz – some people just seem to 'get it' while others can stare and stare without ever working out the secret of the riddle. Those people who heard Jesus reading this passage just turned to each other and said, 'Isn't this old Joseph's boy?' Well, wouldn't you, if the man who made your chairs suddenly claimed to be the Messiah?

If you've got a Bible to hand, you might want to read a bit more of the chapter, because it's heady stuff. Our God is a God who changes things and who wants to see us involved in changing things.

Continental

Sometimes we think God is a spiritual being who isn't concerned about our physical selves; sometimes we think of him as a kind of social and political agenda. He's both. Thank you, God.

Coffee

This passage is a vision of freedom. Jesus identified this passage with his early proclamation of the gospel. Do you feel like you are living a gospel of freedom? How can you begin to live more in the way of Jesus?

Orange Juice

No child will die in infancy; everyone will live to a ripe old age … My people will live in the houses they build; they will enjoy grapes from their own vineyards.

ISAIAH 65:20–21

THE ISAIAH AGENDA

The Big Breakfast

There are so many great passages in Isaiah, it's been hard to choose just a few. This one is my favourite, particularly after I read a little book called *The Isaiah Vision* by Raymond Fung from the World Council of Churches. He says that this passage is a concise description of the kind of world God wants us to live in: children grow up to be adults, the old are healthy and live long, and everyone gets to benefit from the fruits of their labour.

Fung then goes on to say that there are a lot of people in the world today who can agree with this 'Isaiah Agenda' and who we can get alongside and work with in partnership. It's an exciting idea.

When I was a teenager I was still hearing Christians debating about whether a non-Christian could ever do anything good. Now, at last, we can work together for God's Kingdom, even if not everyone knows that's what they're doing! The hope is that when we work with other people who care about the young, the old and those in need of work and housing, they will see something special about us. The question is, what might that be?

Continental

'We want to communicate the following to our neighbours: "The God we believe in is one who protects the children, empowers the elderly, and walks with working men and women. As Christians, we wish to act accordingly. We believe you share in similar concerns. Let us join hands"' (Raymond Fung).

Coffee

Are there people in your neighbourhood or place of work who are doing better than you at bringing about the Isaiah Agenda? How could you bless them? Should you get involved with them?

Orange Juice
The Lord will come down like a whirlwind with his flaming chariots. He will be terribly furious and punish his enemies with fire.

ISAIAH 66:15

HE'LL BE COMING ROUND THE MOUNTAIN ...

The Big Breakfast
'He'll be coming round the mountain when he comes … He'll be wearing pink pyjamas when he comes …' Except here we have the original quote and it actually says, 'He'll be flaming fires of wrath when he comes,' which adds a little twist to things, don't you think?

There's this annoying thing about God: I can go through the whole book of Isaiah picking out all the famous bits, the exciting bits, the nice bits, the challenging bits, but that would be to misrepresent both the book and God. Unfortunately for us, God never conforms to what we want him to be, so while the idea of God as a consuming fire is not exactly *en vogue*, here it is in the Bible.

God gets angry. His anger burns against sin, and many people are gonna get burned. There's no way around this. Even St Paul – a proper saint, no less – said that a good person will get to heaven 'like someone escaping from flames' (1 Corinthians 3:15). We're going to arrive at the Pearly Gates rather warm, and with a faint smell of smoke about us. Like a survivor of a car crash, we will meet God filled with the adrenaline rush of miraculous life, the blood coursing through our veins suddenly audible, and beautiful, and wonderful.

Continental
Many people have criticized Christians for 'making God in their own image', most notably Sigmund Freud. In what ways might you be doing this?

Coffee
Pick up a newspaper or watch the TV news today. What do you think God is angry about?

Orange Juice

It doesn't matter if you are a Greek or a Jew, or if you are circumcised or not. You may even be a barbarian or a Scythian, and you may be a slave or a free person. Yet Christ is all that matters, and he lives in all of us.

COLOSSIANS 3:11

POLITICS AND RELIGION?

The Big Breakfast

There are some things that Christians don't talk about, like the fact that in every Western country ethnic minorities end up with their own churches. Or the fact that Christianity is now a Southern Hemisphere religion, with white people in a minority. Or the fact that not so long ago, in South Africa and parts of the USA, racism was taught as a 'biblical' principle.

Well, we know the reasons for that, and we don't need to dig them up. But we do need to think Christianly about issues of race. By the middle of the century, those from a European ethnic background will be in a minority in the USA, so we gotta get wise sooner or later.

So we must start from the baseline. And the baseline isn't just that we are all made equal (I defy anyone to show me how God has made one person to be of lesser worth in his sight than another): the 'here' that Paul is talking about in this verse is the church – God's universal church throughout the world. There is no such thing as a black church, a white church, an Asian church – there is only God's church, where these differences disappear. It makes John Lennon's song 'Imagine' seem a little unambitious really, doesn't it?

Continental

'When the missionaries arrived in Africa the Africans had the land and the missionaries had the Bible. They taught us to pray with our eyes closed. When we opened them they had the land and we had the Bible' (Jomo Kenyatta).

Coffee

Start these few days by searching your own heart. Is there any prejudice that you need to repent of?

Orange Juice

I would gladly be placed under God's curse and be separated from Christ for the good of my own people.

ROMANS 9:3

BELNGING

The Big Breakfast

To say that our racial and ethnic identities should not be too important within the church of God is not to say that they disappear. I am still a European, an Englishman, a Yorkshireman, a Leeds United supporter, etc. These tribal loyalties still have meaning for me, although being a Christian means that I react differently when the crowd at Leeds United starts singing, 'Stand up if you hate Man U'.

Paul was a Christian who had grown up as a devout Jew. Becoming a Christian didn't suddenly turn off his ethnic identity. Instead, his love for his people increased as his own tribal loyalty was amplified by God's love for the Jews. Paul even goes so far as to say he would be willing to sacrifice his own salvation if only the Jews would come to know Jesus.

That's Paul's job: to care for those in his home, his family, his tribe. If he didn't care for them, pray for them, share the gospel with them, then who would? The person who said 'Charity begins at home' wasn't saying that we should look after our own family at the expense of others; rather that we should not ignore those close to hand in our desire to love those on the fringes.

Continental

Becoming a Christian made Paul love his people even more than he had done before. Many Christians love the church so much that they neglect their family and neighbourhood. Christians need to have their feet planted firmly in the soil of their communities, because the church can grow nowhere else.

Coffee

What tribes do you belong to? How can you share Jesus' love with those tribes?

Orange Juice

All of you are part of the same body. There is only one Spirit of God … We have only one Lord, one faith, and one baptism. There is one God who is the Father of all people.

EPHESIANS 4:4-6

ONE

The Big Breakfast

I have a wonderful picture of a friend of mine which I keep in a draw in my office, and when I pull it out it makes me smile. My friend is called Otniel and he's a Romanian pastor. The thing is, Oti (as we liked to call him) was just a guy at college to us, and now he preaches in a *huge* church in Bucharest, with today's verse in three-foot letters above his head in Romanian. If the Baptist Union of Romania ever want to get in touch with me, I've got some great stories!

And that's how I've often heard this verse: it's about baptism, about how you can't get baptized again because there's only one baptism. Yet this is only a small part of what Paul is talking about, which is the church. The Bible's approach to the church is very aggressive on the unity issue, because in Paul's day race was at least as big an issue as it is today. The church had to contend with Jewish Christians, who tended to look down on everyone who wasn't Jewish, Roman citizens, who felt the same about everyone not like them, and a whole mass of Gentiles caught in the middle.

In that situation we need to hear regular teaching on the unity of the church under God. When was the last time you heard a sermon on unity in your church?

Continental

'We're one/ But we're not the same/ We get to carry each other/ Carry each other' (U2, 'One').

Coffee

Why not resolve to visit a church that's really different from your own? If you live in a city you probably have all kinds of options, but even in the country you will find a wide variety.

Orange Juice

'Lord, that's true,' the woman said, 'but even dogs get the crumbs that fall from their owner's table.' Jesus answered, 'Dear woman, you really do have a lot of faith, and you will be given what you want.' **MATTHEW 15:27-28**

DEALING WITH THE REALITY

The Big Breakfast

Jesus really existed. That's the conclusion I have made from this story alone. It's so weird that no one would have made it up. A Gentile (non-Jewish) woman has approached Jesus with a request: would he heal her daughter? They then have this really strange conversation in which Jesus seems to be saying, 'No, I won't heal your daughter because you aren't Jewish, and for me to bless you would be like throwing my best food to the dogs.' We have her answer above, and Jesus was suitably impressed. Presumably Jesus was testing her resolve and perhaps her understanding of the situation: did she know who he was, did she realize the consequences of asking him into her life?

Jesus didn't ignore the real facts of racial prejudice, he didn't act as if there wasn't a problem. That's why he told parables about Samaritans, the most loathed grouping to Jews, because they were Jews who had intermarried outside Judaism. We must follow Jesus' example and not pretend that differences aren't there. They are, and only by facing our differences and celebrating them and our unity under God can we go forward.

Continental

'I want to be the white man's brother, not his brother-in-law' (Martin Luther King).

Coffee

What are the real issues of racial (or other) prejudice in your community? Is there anything you can do to show your solidarity with those experiencing persecution? Pray for an opportunity to get involved, if you dare.

Orange Juice
Do not ill-treat or abuse foreigners who live among you. Remember, you were foreigners in Egypt.

EXODUS 22:21

THE HOTTEST POTATO

The Big Breakfast
This is undoubtedly asking for trouble: write to me via the publisher to tell me what a bad boy I am. You see, I can't get away from the fact that in the Bible there are two key ways of judging how godly a society is: how it treats the fatherless and the husbandless, and how it treats the foreigner, the sojourner, or as we would put it nowadays, the refugee or asylum seeker.

Setting aside how our country treats single mothers and young people in care (God forgive us our cold hearts!), we have to face up to the fact that the way the Bible suggests we treat asylum seekers is not exactly in harmony with what our politicians are suggesting, egged on by right-wing press coverage.

This raises the question of what the role of the church should be in a country that institutionalizes certain acceptable forms of racism. I don't know how to answer that question on a global scale, but in my street about a quarter of the houses are occupied by Asian families: it must be my job to befriend them and help them become part of our community as much as they want to. Perhaps I should speak up for the minorities in my area, and write to my government about asylum issues. What will you do?

Continental
'The Christian with social concern must champion all those who need champions, not just those whose championing is currently popular' (Os Guinness).

Coffee
Next time you read about asylum seekers and refugees, resolve to think differently about them. Ask God how he sees them, and pray for them.

Orange Juice

I pray that the Lord will bless and protect you, and that he will show you mercy and kindness. May the Lord be good to you and give you peace.

NUMBERS 6:24-26

SHALOM

The Big Breakfast

This prayer is the closest we have to a 'Lord's Prayer' of the Old Testament: it's what God tells Aaron (the first Israelite priest) to say as a blessing over the people. It introduces us to a big word in the Old Testament: peace. The Hebrew word is *shalom*, and you will often hear Jewish people greet each other by wishing peace on each other using this ancient word. Likewise, Muslims bless each other with the Arabic *salaam*.

Unfortunately, like our woolly word 'love', 'peace' doesn't really cover the full meaning of *shalom*, which is much, much more than an absence of war or noise. *Shalom* is a big, fat word, encompassing all the desires and aspirations of God's people in the Old Testament. *Shalom* encompasses what we are looking for when we pray, 'Your Kingdom come, your will be done on earth as it is in heaven.'

In different places in the Bible *shalom* can mean 'completeness', 'security', even 'prosperity' (if you have time, have a look at Jeremiah 29:7). So don't underestimate it: this word has all the power of God's first covenant in it. If you're looking for God's plan for how people, communities and nations should live together, *shalom*'s your word. Just as *sözö* encompasses what the New Testament is about, *shalom* pulls together all the major themes of the Old Testament: God's people, God's justice and God's purpose.

Continental

The English word 'peace' brings to mind restfulness and tranquillity, but the Hebrew word *shalom* recognizes that such a state does not come about by accident; neither is it a place you escape to. *Shalom* is truth, justice and righteousness ruling in our world: to get there, we won't have much time for snoozing!

Coffee

Why not pray this blessing for yourself and for others around you today?

Orange Juice
Pray that our Lord will make us strong and give us peace.

PSALM 29:11

IMAGINING SHALOM

The Big Breakfast
Not much from me today. Given yesterday's words, take some time out to let these words from the Psalms soak into you.

Imagine what your world would look like if *shalom* ruled. Pray that this prophetic insight will begin to come true. Ask God how you can be part of his plan. Write down your thoughts in the space below.

Continental
God's peace is not just an individual thing: if he gives his peace to his people, who are they? The church? Your neighbourhood? The people on TV?

Coffee
Do one thing today that will bring more *shalom* into your home or place of work.

Orange Juice

For to us a child is born, to us a son is given, and the government will be on his shoulders. And he will be called Wonderful Counsellor, Mighty God, Everlasting Father, Prince of Peace.

ISAIAH 9:6 NIV

HOPE FOR THE FUTURE

The Big Breakfast

If you've ever been to a Christmas carol service (and most of us have at one time or another), you've probably heard this prophecy about the coming Messiah (it means 'anointed one'). It is quoted in Handel's *Messiah*, full of pomp and with a very jaunty tune. But, of course, later in Isaiah we are reminded that 'He was wounded and crushed because of our sins; by taking our punishment, he made us completely well' (Isaiah 53:5).

Jesus was a bringer of *shalom*, of the Kingdom of God. He came to institute a time of good news, freedom, healing, pardon and God's favour (see Luke 4:18–19). There is a great sense of joy in the words of the prophet: he is full of hope that God is going to do something new and dramatic to bring about the time of *shalom*. And later on, while speaking about God's servant Israel, he is also prophesying about the cost Jesus would pay to begin the in-breaking of *shalom* into our world.

Take yourself back to that carol service. Imagine you're hearing these words for the first time as you wait for your country to be invaded. The dream of God intervening and changing history is so attractive as to be almost unbelievable … Will you believe it?

Continental

Just think on these words for a minute: 'by taking our punishment, he made us completely well'.

Coffee

'Jesus, thank you for all that you did for me in living and dying and rising again. I love you and worship you. I will do my part.'

Orange Juice

I promise that this new temple will be more glorious than the first one. I will also bless this city with peace.

HAGGAI 2:9

PEACE IN THE HOUSE!

The Big Breakfast

Over 2,500 years ago the whole nation of Judah was 'ethnically cleansed' from the land of Palestine and deported *en masse* to Babylon. Seventy years later, under more favourable political conditions, a trickle of Jews began to return, and over the following hundred years the city of Jerusalem and its historic temple and walls were rebuilt. This verse from the prophet Haggai is the centrepiece of his challenge to the Jews in Jerusalem to pull their fingers out and finish what they had started. By the time Haggai was speaking there were perhaps only a handful who would have remembered Solomon's temple which the Babylonians destroyed, but it had already developed a mythological status as the pinnacle of Jewish culture and worship. The idea that God would ever do something greater than what he had done in the time of David and Solomon was just ridiculous!

Yet here's Haggai – and God – telling us that God has even bigger plans. We know from history that the second temple was paltry in comparison to the first, but it did see a period of political freedom for the Jews, when the Maccabees fought for Jewish independence and cleansed the temple in 167 BC. Maybe there's a clue here about *shalom*.

Continental

'I tell you for certain that if you have faith in me, you will do the same things that I am doing. You will do even greater things …' (John 14:12).

Coffee

Shalom clearly has political implications. What might they be for you?

Orange Juice
I solemnly promise to bless the people of Israel with unending peace. I will protect them and let them become a powerful nation … I will live among my people and be their God.

EZEKIEL 37:26–27

THE REAL DEAL

The Big Breakfast
For me, the phrase, 'I will live among my people and be their God' is at the centre of *shalom*. It's something that you find all over the Bible, this idea that at the heart of God's plans is the simple desire for relationship.

Sometimes God has been pictured as having no feelings, or even as being incapable of feeling, yet this hunger to be with his people seems to be more than just a picture of God. Ultimately words are only a grasping after God, but a word like *shalom* can signal for us a whole area of God's character. When you think of peace in future, think big!

What would it mean for you to make a *covenant* – a binding agreement – of peace with God? God has already outlined his side of the deal: it will be for ever, it will result in multiplication, and God will live with you. What's your side of the deal?

Continental
'You will never find peace and happiness until you are ready to commit yourself to something worth dying for' (Jean-Paul Sartre).

Coffee
Over the last 10 days you have been looking at two words that add up God's ideas of wholeness. Write down one thing you have learnt, one thing you will pray for, and one thing you want to change about your circumstances as a result of the stuff you've read.

Orange Juice

He makes grass grow for the cattle, and plants for man to cultivate –
bringing forth food from the earth: wine that gladdens the heart of man, oil
to make his face shine, and bread that sustains his heart.

PSALM 104:14–15 NIV

THE BIBLE AND
THE BOOZE

The Big Breakfast

Imagine you are about to lead worship in your
local church or with some Christian friends. You
decide to thank God for all the good things in
your world. How many of you would put wine near the top
of your list?

So where do we start? We have to start at the beginning,
surprisingly enough. My beginning is the question that is on
most people's lips: 'Is the Bible really as down on alcohol as
many Christians seem to think it is?' Well, the answer is
undoubtedly NO. Wine is good – from God, even. And it's
good not only because it was the only way to disinfect water
(true), nor just because it was the easiest drink to make
(almost true), nor because it tastes nice. None of the above:
it's good because it 'gladdens the heart of man'! What a great
way of putting it.

When I walk round Leeds on a Saturday night I don't
comment to myself, 'Oh, look at the gang of lads whose
hearts are so clearly gladdened by lager!' But we'll come back
to that soon. The place to start is that alcohol is not just OK,
it is a gift from God, and he is to be praised for it. (More on
this later, so don't jump to conclusions!)

Continental

'Our bodies are not
puritanical. The
pleasant habits of
eating and drinking
were never meant to
be subject to a
chemical equation'
(Lord Horder, British
Royal Physician).

Coffee

What are the good things about food and drink that you can thank God for?
We don't do it very often, so make time to say thank you for all that you enjoy.

Orange Juice
It isn't clever to get drunk! Drinking makes a fool of you and leads to fights.

PROVERBS 20:1

TAKE TWO ...

The Big Breakfast
Being 'mature' is normally an insult for anyone under 30, but that has to be our way. In my view, holding yesterday's and today's readings in tension is what being mature is all about. I read the other day that a current craze in Absinthe drinking is rapidly dying out because its main enthusiasts – young lads who think that drinking a 70%-proof drink is somehow 'cool' – usually end up nearly dying in hospital. We can all see that for what it is. If you drink, try going to a party and staying sober to see whether or not alcohol is a mocker and a brawler.

But in many ways, building a wall around alcohol can be just as immature: it's a tacit acknowledgement that we can't be trusted with a bottle of beer in our hand. If that statement is true, then we have a problem, which some of us do. Addiction or domestic violence may lead us to steer clear for personal reasons. But for the rest of us, following Jesus in a grown-up way means becoming victim neither to alcohol nor to the fear of it.

Continental
'I have better use for my brain than to poison it with alcohol. To put alcohol in the human brain is like putting sand in the bearings of an engine' (Thomas Edison).

Coffee
If you have a Bible, try reading Proverbs 23:29–35, for more of the same. There's no way to get away from the Bible's message that getting drunk is totally wrong – and stupid, to boot!

Orange Juice

John the Baptist did not go around eating and drinking, and you said, 'John has a demon in him!' But because the Son of Man goes around eating and drinking, you say, 'Jesus eats and drinks too much! He is even a friend of tax collectors and sinners.'

LUKE 7:33-34

WINE IS NOT THE ONLY DRINK

The Big Breakfast

Jesus had a hard time of it right from the beginning, and one of the key ways in which he offended lots of people was by not conforming to the stereotype of what a religious person should be like. Jesus is almost raising his hands to the sky and saying, 'I can't win with you people! Too godly, and I get called a freak; too worldly, and I get called a hypocrite.'

But I have to admit that there are other situations in which I might feel a bit more like the Pharisees. For example, take my friend Katie (not her real name). From the age of about 15, Katie started going out to parties with guys a lot older than her. She was particularly fond of spontaneous, probably illegal house parties. While Katie chose not to drink, I still had that feeling that she would somehow 'catch' the sin in such a place.

In truth, we only catch what we want to. If you and God are together on your drinking, then let people know that the decisions you are making are not made on your own. But don't try to kid yourself about what God thinks, because that road only leads to one place.

Continental

Why is it that no Christian ever gets drunk? I have picked Christians up out of the gutter, who the next day have assured me they were 'only a little tipsy'.

Coffee

If you drink alcohol, can you agree a daily limit with God (and maybe with a friend or two who can help you)? If you don't, think through what your attitude should be to those who do.

Orange Juice

Don't destroy yourself by getting drunk, but let the Spirit fill your life.

EPHESIANS 5:18

GOD – THE LOW-ALCOHOL ALTERNATIVE

The Big Breakfast

I've got into the fourth day without declaring my colours, but now the time has come for me to look you straight in the eye and tell you where I stand. Well, sort of. To be honest, I don't know where I stand. I haven't drunk any alcohol (except for the odd glass of champagne at weddings) since I was a teenager, but I don't try to make a biblical argument for my position.

Because I grew up in a family in which alcohol was not a positive influence (let's leave it at that ...), and because I found myself *extremely* fond of sweet cider at the age of about 15, I decided that I wanted to give it up. It's not a big sacrifice and I don't go on about it to other people. I just think that it ruins people and makes multinationals rich.

When I ask Christians why they drink more than they probably should, they normally talk about how it helps them to be more friendly and open, less inhibited. If you know someone who has recently become a Christian, you probably get the feeling that they are 'on something': animated, disinhibited, gregarious ... Read the verse again and pray that God will fill you with his Holy Spirit. No hangovers!

Continental

'Without the Spirit of God we can do nothing but add sin to sin' (John Wesley).

Coffee

Do nothing today, but ask God for a fresh infilling of his Spirit.

Orange Juice

It is best not to eat meat or drink wine or do anything else that causes problems for other followers of the Lord.

ROMANS 14:21

A WAY THROUGH THE WOODS

The Big Breakfast

Paul had a big problem in the early church. There were some Christians who felt that food that had been offered to idols was untouchable for Christians, because it had effectively been given to a demon. Then there were some who felt that because Jesus was Lord of all, eating that food would have no effect on them.

The argument between them was long and loud, and Paul was clearly on the side of the 'liberals'. I reckon Paul today would probably have enjoyed a pint or two, just like his Lord Jesus. However, he talks to the people who agree with him and says a funny thing: 'Don't do it.' Why?

If you read the whole of this chapter in the Bible, you will find that while Paul sees that we have a great deal of freedom under Jesus, we shouldn't always take advantage of that freedom. One reason for not doing what we feel like is the way it will affect other Christians: if you are going to lose a Christian brother or sister over your drinking, you'd better feel sure that you are standing on principle for a good reason. There are a million things more important than your alcohol consumption.

Continental

'Prejudice is a great time saver. It enables you to form opinions without bothering to get the facts' (anonymous).

Coffee

Is there someone who you disagree with over this issue? How can you show them that they matter to you, whatever your difference of opinion?

Orange Juice

When the builders had finished laying the foundation of the temple, the priests put on their robes and blew trumpets in honour of the LORD, while the Levites from the family of Asaph praised God with cymbals. **EZRA 3:10**

CELEBRATING WORK

The Big Breakfast

Here's a verse from the story of Ezra (told in more detail on pp. 49–53) which comes just as the foundation of the new temple has been laid. When I read this passage I tend to focus on the worshippers, which is natural, but today I want to remember the builders, as we start five days thinking about work – something which will take up a huge part of our lives but which is painfully untalked-about in our churches.

When was the last time your church got a choir and orchestra out to celebrate your work? You're probably aware that your church is not alone in making little of the work that you do. In many cases, the person who works long hours or doesn't help out at church because they're tired is made to feel guilty that their job is in the way.

I'm not saying my church is that different, it's just that I'd like it to be different. If we're going to have to live in a society where you can't eat or get a roof over your head without working 40 hours a week in a job you don't like, then let's at least find ways of working that we can celebrate as Christians.

Continental

'As we turn away from the flagstaff where the new banner has just been run up; as we depart, our ears yet ringing with the blare of the herald's trumpets that have proclaimed the new order of things, what shall we turn to then, what *must* we turn to then? To what else, save our work, our daily labour?' (William Morris).

Coffee

Has God called you to the job that you're in? Are you able to see him at work through you as you work? Are you able to glorify God through your work? If the answer to all these questions is yes, thank God for a wonderful job. If the answer to all three is no, pray and check the local paper! Seriously, let these questions percolate through your mind as you talk to God about your work.

Orange Juice

I got whatever I wanted and did whatever made me happy. But most of all, I enjoyed my work. Then I thought about everything I had done, including the hard work, and it was simply chasing the wind. ***ECCLESIASTES 2:10–11***

THE DARK SIDE

The Big Breakfast

If the writer of Ecclesiastes was alive today, he would probably be in a band like Nirvana or Radiohead, making music that was simultaneously beautifully melancholic and dangerously suicidal.

I have had all kinds of jobs in my time, but only once have I felt that my job was like 'chasing after the wind'. I had to work to get money, and ended up working in a call centre. At this job I met people who appeared to be just like me, except that they seemed to have a part of them missing: they seemed to have the life sucked out of them, they had become part of the machine.

We should never underestimate the power of a job to shape our lives. A really good job, and we come home energized and full of hope. A really bad job, and ...well, you've read the verses above. A good job is not necessarily a well-paid one, and a bad job is not necessarily a poorly-paid one. You might be simply in the wrong kind of job, or feeling trapped into a certain kind of work by financial pressures. If that's the case, try to find someone who can help you with careers or debt advice: never let these things rule you, because if they do, then God can't.

Continental

'The trouble with the rat race is that, even if you win, you're still a rat' (Lily Tomlin).

Coffee

Identify the hard bits in your job and give them over to God. If you feel that they outweigh the easy bits by too much, you may need to get out if you can. Draw up a three-year plan to get to where you want to be, and share it with God.

Orange Juice

Do your work willingly, as though you were serving the Lord himself, and not just your earthly master. In fact, the Lord Christ is the one you are really serving, and you know that he will reward you. *COLOSSIANS 3:23-24*

THE LIGHT SIDE

The Big Breakfast

I once had a really surreal weekend listening to two different Christian speakers at two different events. Amazingly, both were talking about work. Less surprising was the fact that they didn't agree. The first speaker said that because God wants us to be happy and fulfilled, we should look for a new job if we are unhappy in our present one. We just need to find a place where we can be fruitful. The other speaker said that leaving a job without God's permission is an act of unfaithfulness to God, and that we should do everything in our power to make our job work.

The second speaker spoke from this passage particularly, and I guess I can see where he was coming from. In our society, there are lots of jobs that just need doing, like stacking shelves and answering phone calls, and they are never going to be particularly exciting.

Sometimes we have to let go of our desire for money and prestige, and focus on pleasing God (and our employer) by working hard where we are. Who knows, if you work 'as for the Lord', you'll probably shine and get a promotion!

Continental

'A dairymaid can milk cows to the glory of God' (Martin Luther).

Coffee

What can you do today that will be for God?

Orange Juice

We didn't waste our time being lazy, and we didn't accept food from anyone without paying for it. We didn't want to be a burden to any of you, so night and day we worked as hard as we could. *2 THESSALONIANS 3:7-8*

IF YOU CAN, YOU SHOULD

The Big Breakfast

Every now and then, normally at the annual Greenbelt festival here in the UK, I meet people who call themselves 'Christian anarchists'. Some of them are very serious political theorists and some of them are looking for a revolution. Then there are those – less likely to be Christians, it's true – who just object to working. Sorry, guys, but you can get away with that only because the rest of us are supporting you – either rich parents or taxpayers through the benefits system. Not right, not fair, not biblical.

Well, that's Paul's view, anyway. When a visiting preacher from far away comes to Leeds where I live, he doesn't go straight to the Jobcentre, because he expects to get paid (although we might dress this up in religious language). Paul's not massively into this freeloading culture. Perhaps he wants to maintain his independence, so that his hearers know that he is preaching the true message and not what anyone is paying to hear.

I don't know, but he seems quite proud of his financial independence. He probably should be: I'm certainly impressed. What it means for paid clergy today, I don't know, but it definitely means we should work if we can.

Continental

'The reward of labour is *life* … the reward of creation' (William Morris).

Coffee

Do you feel that you are working productively in your life? Try to answer the question on three levels: material, relational and spiritual. Can you become more productive?

Orange Juice
And on the seventh day hold a sacred assembly and do no regular work.

LEVITICUS 23:8 NIV

STOP IT!

The Big Breakfast
Some of us have the problem that work just gets in the way of our life; for others work is their life. Such people have a tendency to look down on the work-to-rule nine-to-fivers as weak-willed slackers. They understand the meaning of *real* work – except, of course, they know nothing about life. That's the terrible problem of the professional classes in the West: men and women who spend their whole lives working in order to build a family that's falling apart through neglect. God knew what he was doing when he instituted the sabbath.

It's so annoying. Imagine it's harvest-time and the corn is ripe. You go out and begin harvesting, but then the sun goes down and it's Friday night. You *have* to stop for 24 hours, or else you'd be breaking the law. It's maddening! A few weeks ago I went on holiday and took my computer with me to try and finish this book. Only I didn't: by a string of coincidences it never got into the car, so I had two weeks of holiday in which I couldn't do any work. It was wonderful!

We need to learn what 'sabbath' means for us today. God's priorities on that day began with him, but included family and community as well. How can we get that time back? We need it if we are ever going to change our country.

Continental
'No one has yet said, on their deathbed, "I wish I'd spent more time at the office"' (anonymous).

Coffee
What does your sabbath look like? Do you need to make more space for yourself, friends, family, God? Why not ask God what your priorities should be?

Orange Juice
They told me, 'Those captives who have come back are having all kinds of troubles. They are terribly disgraced, Jerusalem's walls are broken down, and its gates have been burnt.'

NEHEMIAH 1:3

THE BROKEN-DOWN CITY

The Big Breakfast
Once upon a time, Ezra and Nehemiah were one book. The reason why they were separated is lost in the mists of time, but one reason might be that Nehemiah is mainly written in the first person by Nehemiah himself. Nehemiah was 'cup-bearer to the King', which might not sound much to us, but it made him a relatively big cheese in the world of Jewish slaves.

For reasons undisclosed, Nehemiah has not joined his countrymen in the rebuilding of Jerusalem, and only hears about the city's terrible state when one of his brothers visits him and explains that the walls are in ruins. Nehemiah doesn't know what to do, but his boss, King Artaxerxes, sees that Nehemiah is sad. Being sad in the King's presence was generally a beheading offence, but instead Artaxerxes asks Nehemiah what's up, and before long our narrator has been made governor of Judah.

There are lots of stories like this in the Bible: some nobody suddenly becomes important. What's the secret? Well, I think it might have something to do with the fact that Nehemiah obeyed God but also acknowledged the authority of the King. He didn't run away from his responsibilities, and because he respected the worldly power over him, he was rewarded by the King and was used by God.

Continental
'Do your work willingly, as though you were serving the Lord himself, and not just your earthly master' (Colossians 3:23).

Coffee
Nehemiah was 'cupbearer to the King'. What roles do you have in your life? How can you honour both God and the people who have authority over you in those roles?

Orange Juice

We must honour our God by the way we live, so the Gentiles can't find fault with us … Now give back the fields, vineyards, olive orchards, and houses you have taken and also the interest you have been paid.

NEHEMIAH 5:9–14

The Big Breakfast

Judah was famine-stricken, and in order to buy food from outside the country the people needed money. They mortgaged their property to the few rich Jews that there were and ended up in trouble because of the huge interest that was being exacted. Nehemiah was having none of this. 'We've just got all these people out of slavery, and you want to make them slaves again,' he says. The nobles agree and give the money back. Jubilee 2000 in action!

Then, after the first example of debt cancellation, comes the first example of 'fair trade'. Well, not quite, to be honest, but it's close! The governor of Judah was entitled to live on the choicest foods that were available to him, all 'paid for' by tribute, which meant that all the people had to give him their best produce as a form of taxation. Nehemiah records that he and all his family refused this food so that the people who had grown it could eat it and benefit from the fruits of their labours. They agreed to pay for their own food so that everyone got a fair deal.

Sometimes people see these campaigns for social justice as modern inventions. Those people need to read their Bibles a bit more.

Continental

Borrowing money and shopping are both deeply spiritual and moral activities. They are both very easy to do. How can you shop and spend more justly?

Coffee

Does God want you to intervene in a social issue of which you are aware? Spend some time listening to him.

Orange Juice

Our enemies were trying to frighten us and to keep us from our work. But I asked God to give me strength.

NEHEMIAH 6:9

CAPE FEAR

The Big Breakfast

We're back to the enemies of Judah again, I'm afraid. I wish, somewhere in the Bible, it said, 'And once you become a Christian everything will be SUPER TWINKY' (to quote a T-shirt my friend has) – but, of course, it doesn't. This time the bad guys are trying to stop the rebuilding of the walls, and it's a great illustration of how the enemy has a go at us: (1) He wants us to be afraid, so that (2) we will get discouraged and (3) God's work won't get done. It's a pretty simple tactic. Sports people always talk about the psychology leading up to big matches and fights. The best thing you can do is to get the opposition afraid of you.

So what's Nehemiah's response? 'Lord, finish the work off for us so we don't have to be in danger'? Nope. 'Lord, make the bad guys go away so that we'll be safe'? *Nada. Non. Nein danke.* Nehemiah prays that God will give him the strength to keep going, whatever. Scumbag!

If you read through the whole of Nehemiah you'll see that he often talks to God, as if to say, 'I did this for you, so you'd better back me up.' And it's true: he takes the tough decisions in a way that our modern politicians could only dream about.

Continental

'Learn to be patient, so that you will please God and be given what he has promised' (Hebrews 10:36).

Coffee

If you are in a situation where you are afraid, or seemingly not achieving what you set out to achieve, just repeat Nehemiah's prayer: 'Now strengthen my hands' (Nehemiah 6:9 NIV).

Orange Juice

… when [Ezra] opened the book, they all stood up. Ezra praised the great Lord God, and the people shouted, 'Amen! Amen!' Then they bowed with their faces to the ground and worshipped the Lord. **NEHEMIAH 8:5–6**

THE BIG BOOK

The Big Breakfast

Books, eh? Who needs 'em nowadays, what with radio, TV, computers, mobile phones and all the rest? What funny things they are, bits of paper stuck together with words on them. I get my news on my super-light-fits-in-my-pocket home multimedia washing machine.

Books. Apparently we live in a 'non-book culture'. Oh dear, you're so out of fashion reading this, then, aren't you! Put it down right away, you can't possibly learn anything from it!

The Book. How would you start a big party? A book reading? Well, perhaps not. Here's old man Ezra back at the helm at the beginning of the city of Jerusalem's celebrations at the completion of the wall. I'm sure that if there'd been fireworks and the Spice Girls they would have been there too, but this bit would always have come first: a book reading.

And what a book. Ezra reads The Law, The Pentateuch, the first five books of the Bible!!!! And as he opens the book (well, scroll, probably), what's the people's response? They praise God!

Continental

A famous guy once said, 'When one has tired of London, one has tired of life.' I think Ezra and Nehemiah would have echoed Psalm 119 and said, 'When one has tired of the Scriptures, one has tired of God.'

Coffee

If you have a favourite Bible verse, read it through and remember how much joy you have received through reading the Scriptures. If you are finding the Bible dull and dry at the moment, and it's not just my fault for being boring, pray that God will inject some passion into the next time you pick up a Bible.

Orange Juice

Everyone who had returned from Babylonia built shelters. They lived in them and joyfully celebrated the Festival of Shelters for the first time since the days of Joshua son of Nun.

NEHEMIAH 8:17

The Big Breakfast

The funny thing about the Old Testament is that everybody thinks it was a really terrible time and nobody ever had any fun. But boy, did these guys know how to party.

You've probably heard of the 'tithe', because Christians often use the term to mean that they should give 10% of their income to God's service. In Nehemiah's day, it was a bit more complicated than that. In addition to the tithe (which I'll come back to in a moment), there were two other kinds of offerings: one for the poor and one for anyone who worked for the city (including priests, choirs and soldiers). So, if other offerings covered community service and supporting the priesthood, what was the tithe for?

Parties. The tithe (which was a tenth) was used for temple worship, particularly the special feast days. All this stuff was given over to God on days like the Day of Atonement and, if this isn't too irreverent, it must have been chaos. (Veggies, miss this sentence out.) Animals being slaughtered everywhere, blood running through the temple courts … Nehemiah had two full-time choirs that sang in the temple: the noise must have been incredible! There was always time to celebrate God.

Continental

'The Worship of God is not a rule of safety – it is an adventure of the spirit, a flight after the unattainable' (A. N. Whitehead).

Coffee

If you normally have a quiet time with God, why not try having a loud time, and vice versa?

Orange Juice
'You know that we Jews are not allowed to have anything to do with other people. But God has shown me that he doesn't think anyone is unclean or unfit.'

ACTS 10:28

THE WEIRDEST VISION

The Big Breakfast
This is one of my favourite stories in the Bible, which I consider to contain one of the greatest miracles in the Bible. Hopefully you'll agree with me by the end!

Peter is staying at a friend's house, waiting for his dinner to be served. He's starving! Going out onto the roof of the house, he has a vision of all the wee beasties that are forbidden him by the Old Testament law. God then tells him that he should eat all of it. It's almost impossible to explain how shocking this message from God is: because nearly every taboo has been broken and we are so unshockable, the only modern equivalent I can think of would be for God to ask a parent to invite the local paedophile round to babysit.

But Peter gets the message: in matters to do with what is acceptable to God, God decides, not us. As the vision ends and Peter goes downstairs to eat, he finds that a messenger has arrived from a Roman called Cornelius, who wants Peter to visit him. Instead of saying, 'Euch, nasty Gentile, I'm not going,' he learns the message from the vision and goes to see Cornelius. This is his opening speech, and it's impressive. Peter was willing to reject hundreds of years of Jewish culture because God was showing him that he was doing something new.

Continental
God is a God who breaks down boundaries. What boundaries are there between you and your church and the people who live around you? Are there some people who are unwelcome in your church, or, more likely, people who just don't fit in? What does this message say to us today?

Coffee
Pray for someone you know who's very different from you. Pray that God will bless them and that he will show you how to share God with them.

Orange Juice

While Peter was still speaking, the Holy Spirit took control of everyone who was listening. Some Jewish followers of the Lord had come with Peter, and they were surprised that the Holy Spirit had been given to Gentiles.

ACTS 10:44–45

GOD BREAKS THE RULES

The Big Breakfast

Peter discovers that Cornelius wants to hear about Jesus, so he does one of his instant evangelistic talks, which you can read in the preceding verses. Then, much to Peter's surprise, God starts working with these 'unclean' Gentiles before they've even been baptized!

I help to lead a church called REVIVE, made up mainly of young people aged about 16 to 30. We're not particularly big – there's about 60 of us – but we love being together and God seems to be using us. The church grew out of a youth group in which God did some great stuff. Our existence now as a separate congregation is partly due to the fact that we started doing things differently. Fortunately, even though the young people who began getting involved in REVIVE didn't always fit into what church people were meant to be like, our Pastor could see what God was doing and encouraged us.

This is really important today, in a world where there are so many different cultures, because we are no longer going to be able to tell who is a Christian just because they are 'like us'. Discerning what God is up to will become a very important gift in the church of the future. And maybe we should expect to see God doing stuff we just didn't expect!

Continental

God can do things we don't even pray for; his dreams are so much bigger than ours.

Coffee

Pray that God will show you what he's doing in your neck of the woods today, and how he wants you to be involved. Be on the lookout for the Holy Spirit!

Orange Juice

The apostles and the followers in Judea heard that Gentiles had accepted God's message. So when Peter came to Jerusalem, some of the Jewish followers started arguing with him.

ACTS 11:1-2

THE PRICE OF OBEDIENCE

The Big Breakfast

Whenever God does something new, you can guarantee that it will be his own people who will resist it. It's so depressing that a bunch of people who had actually met Jesus could have turned following him into a religion within a few years of Pentecost.

The Jewish Christians just couldn't get their heads round the idea that you could follow Yahweh – their God – without being just like them. They were mad with Peter for eating what would have been unclean food, never mind baptizing a bunch of people who weren't even proper Jews!

Reading about these people causes me some sadness, even though I know this story has a happy ending, because I have met sincere Christians who condemn REVIVE because we do things differently. They don't ask about what we believe, about how many people come along or about the work we do on the streets of Leeds or in the local prison. Because we dress differently, worship differently and act differently, there's something wrong with us. That's an attitude I've got to challenge in the name of Jesus. So there.

Continental

I confess here in print that I often struggle with both hyper-charismatic churches and deeply liturgical churches. I suppose that makes me middle-of-the-road in some ways, but it also makes me like you, probably. Just because we like a way of doing church doesn't make it *the* right way, and just because we don't like another way doesn't make it a wrong way.

Coffee

Have you ever judged a fellow-Christian too harshly because of the differences between you? Take time to say sorry to God and to think about whether you need to sort out the issue.

Orange Juice

And so, my friends, I don't think we should place burdens on the Gentiles who are turning to God.

ACTS 15:19

THE MIRACLE

The Big Breakfast

It's a few chapters later in Acts, and there's been so much rumpus about the Gentiles that the leaders in Jerusalem have called a special meeting to decide what to do (see, some things never change – there'll always be meetings). The same Jewish Christians who were objecting to what God was doing yesterday have heard about everything that's happened and are stunned into silence.

Then the miracle happens. James, Jesus' brother and the appointed leader of the Jewish Christians, speaks for them: 'I don't think we should place burdens on the Gentiles who are turning to God.'

It sounds so easy. Yet what it actually meant was one of the most amazing sacrifices in Bible history. These Jewish Christians were willing to say to the Gentiles, 'We think you're great. We have all this tradition which we love, but we realize it doesn't mean a thing to you, so don't worry about it too much. Just love Jesus with all your hearts, and that makes you our brothers and sisters.'

Continental

God's ideal is that becoming a Christian and following Jesus should be the most natural thing that's ever happened to us. When it isn't that easy, let's be honest and start looking at ourselves first and leave God and the Bible out of it. They're easy to blame for our failure to reach out because they're such big targets, and they don't seem to mind being blamed for the sin of the world.

Coffee

Remember a time when someone you knew helped you to grow in God. Think about what it was about them that made getting closer to God seem easy. Thank God for that person and think about how you can encourage another person in the same way.

Orange Juice

It seemed good to the Holy Spirit and to us not to burden you with anything beyond the following requirements: You are to abstain from food sacrificed to idols, from blood, from the meat of strangled animals and from sexual immorality.

ACTS 15:28–29 NIV

A LETTER OF LOVE

The Big Breakfast

OK, so yesterday I made it sound easy. Well, it wasn't. It *was* a church meeting, after all. The general 'Love Jesus, do what you want' message was tempered a little – just a little. I think this letter tells us that when we look at our own (or another's) tradition, we should be able to put it into three categories:

Firstly, the cultural stuff. That's all the stuff we do that defines us, and we do it because we like it. Surprisingly enough, that seems to have included about 99% of the Jewish law. Secondly, those things that *are* cultural, but which cause us so much offence that we'd rather you didn't do them so that we can be on good terms. Thirdly, the letter prohibits sexual immorality, which is something that has been a key part of following Yahweh from day one. Perhaps this represents those things that are completely non-negotiable.

It's worth remembering that the very same people, so generous over these issues, were rock solid when it came to issues of faith and doctrine: their permission to innovate in the cultural arena was not a permission to innovate in others. God's truth was the rock on which all was built.

Continental

Often we get caught up in judging people according to the strangest criteria. This story teaches us that any way of judging someone other than by seeing their devotion to God and the activity of the Holy Spirit in their lives is – to bring Bill and Ted into the equation – bogus.

Coffee

The generosity of the Jewish Christians was huge. Pray for a heart as full of grace so that you can give to others today.

Orange Juice

Jeremiah, I am your Creator, and before you were born, I chose you to speak for me to the nations.

JEREMIAH 1:5

HE KNOWS, YOU KNOW

The Big Breakfast

It's difficult talking about being 'called', because for some people God writes stuff in the sky, and for others, they spend their whole life seemingly trying to make the right decisions in the dark, without any help from the great careers adviser in the heavens. For me the greatest moments of call could nearly all be put down to fascinating coincidences, so I probably sit somewhere in the middle between the miracle merchants and the rest of us.

I've got two kids on the way (they'll be born by the time you read this), and because their mum has been ill, loads of people have been praying for them. Funnily enough, one thing that all that prayer won't have changed is God's view of them. He knows them already, he knew them even before they were a ball of cells. When they get to know God, he will be introducing himself to people he knows really well: like a Spice Girls fan finally meeting the band, God has loved us like crazy even before we knew who he was.

That is the starting point for Jeremiah and it's the starting point for us, too. He knows us better than we know ourselves, so maybe he might have a good idea of what use he could put us to…

Continental

'Why was I chosen?' [asked Frodo]. 'Such questions cannot be answered,' said Gandalf. 'You may be sure that it was not for any merit that others do not possess: not for power or wisdom at any rate. But you have been chosen, and you must therefore use such strength and heart and wits as you have.' (J. R. R. Tolkien, *The Lord of the Rings*.)

Coffee

Just think about how much God knows you and loves you, and thank him.

Orange Juice
I replied, 'I'm not a good speaker, LORD, and I'm too young.'

JEREMIAH 1:6

THE WAYNE'S WORLD EFFECT

The Big Breakfast
It's one of my favourite movie moments. Wayne and Garth and friends are piled into a tiny car listening to Queen's 'Bohemian Rhapsody'. As the heavy bit at the end of the song kicks in, the entire ensemble headbangs in time to the music. Sublime. Wayne and Garth introduced a variety of stupid phrases into the English language in 1990s, the two most common of which were 'Not!' and 'We're not worthy!'

This latter was used whenever our two anti-heroes got remotely near anyone even mildly famous. Sad, sad, sad – but then, I guess that was the idea. I suppose doing it in front of God is a bit more excusable, but Jeremiah's whining is not a good start. After God has said, (a) 'I know you' and (b) 'I want to use you', Jerry decides to act dumb, literally.

Why can't he speak? Because he's young. Some things never change. I've been in churches where a 25-year-old dealing millions on the stock market is handing out notice sheets. Church must be the only place in the world where youth and energy are signs that we should not be trusted with anything important, and what's worse is that we believe it, just like Jeremiah. 'Oh no, I couldn't be a leader, I'm under 40. Why don't I sit at the back and start a burping competition?'

Continental
'We know that God is always at work for the good of everyone who loves him. They are the ones God has chosen for his purpose …' (Romans 8:28).

Coffee
Are there things that you are afraid of doing because of how others perceive you? It may not be age, but some other prejudice or insecurity. Talk to God about your own fears or any barriers that others may be putting in your way.

Orange Juice

'Don't say you're too young,' the LORD answered. 'If I tell you to go and speak to someone, then go! And when I tell you what to say, don't leave out a word! …'

JEREMIAH 1:7

TOUGHING IT OUT

The Big Breakfast

God's response to our traditional 'I can't do it!' is threefold. I've tried to think of three words that all begin with the same letter, but sadly my mind just doesn't work that way. Also, sadly, the first of these three responses is not 'There, there, never mind, I'll go find someone else to do my work.' In fact, God's reply to Jeremiah is positively rude! 'It's no use moaning,' says God, 'because I've chosen you, and that's that. Or do you want to try disobeying me?'

I think that sometimes Christians imagine that they can hide their lives in a dark corner of the world and be pretty much ignored by God. Pour souls! How wrong can they be? We all know that the shepherd comes and looks for the one lost sheep, wherever it may have got to (Matthew 18:12). It's the same with us: if God has a job for us to do, it's ours and we can't run away from it. There's absolutely no escape from God. That's why it's always advisable never to say 'never' to God: he has a funny way of picking you up on those things.

When you ask most Christians who've done amazing things for God, they will nearly all tell you the same story, and I think that might be the key to greatness: not any special gifting, just the ability to be faithful to God in the place where he's put you.

Continental

'To obey God is perfect liberty' (Seneca).

Coffee

What are the things that you say 'never' about? Can you? Talk to God about what it's all about: fear, stubbornness, selfishness. Be honest, and give him time to speak to you.

Orange Juice
I promise to be with you and keep you safe, so don't be afraid.

JEREMIAH 1:8

YOU'RE NOT ALONE

The Big Breakfast
The other day I took my mum to see an evangelistic comedy magician. It sounds terrible, doesn't it? Actually, he was really good, especially the trick he did which showed Uri Geller to be – ahem! – not quite what he pretends to be. Anyway, at the end of the evening my mum explains why she doesn't want to go to church, and I know that I'm supposed to say something wise and spiritual at this point. Instead, my mouth goes dry and my tongue sticks to the roof of my mouth.

You see, my mum knows everything about me. She knows what a hypocrite I am, that I always took so long with the washing up that she would give up on me and do it herself, that my bedroom door had 'Do not enter: health hazard' stickers on it for a reason. How can I tell her how to sort her life out when mine still seems to be in a mess? I just felt so alone.

The second response God makes to us after we try to run away from his call is to let us know that his work is a partnership. I would never advise anyone to serve God alone (Jesus never sent anyone out on their own), but if it happens, God promises to be closer than a friend, closer than a mother, closer than breathing.

Continental
'I won't leave you like orphans. I will come back to you' (John 14:18).

Coffee
Try this simple exercise as a form of prayer: imagine yourself in a situation in which you are scared to acknowledge you are a Christian. Now imagine Jesus is standing right next to you. Pray that you can be aware of Jesus with you wherever you go.

Orange Juice

The LORD reached out his hand, then he touched my mouth and said, 'I am giving you the words to say …'

JEREMIAH 1:9

OPEN WIDE …!

The Big Breakfast

God doesn't just expect us to obey him, whatever. He doesn't just promise to be with us when we're in scary situations. He also takes us as we are and helps us deal with our issues (even if they seem a lot bigger to us than they are to him).

Of course Jeremiah could speak, but God took his fears seriously and showed him that right where he was weakest, God would use him. This makes sense to me. If I don't keep in touch with God every day, I soon start to do things on my own, with no 'need' to consult God or ask him for help. It takes a crisis to get me out of this mess: I suddenly remember that things run better with God in control, and I try my best to put him back into the driver's seat.

Now, in a situation in which I'm completely out of my depth, there's no chance of me either doing it on my own, or getting the glory for any success. God comes out of things best when he uses people like Gideon, who became an army leader despite being a bit of a … well, I won't be rude to a Bible hero, but you get the idea. So join the local Dangerous Sports Club now, because Christianity is the most dangerous of them all!

Continental

'God chose the foolish things of this world to put the wise to shame. He chose the weak things of this world to put the powerful to shame' (1 Corinthians 1:27).

Coffee

What do you need to serve God effectively in what he's called you to do? Go on, just ask him – it's OK!

Orange Juice

What a beautiful sight! On the mountains a messenger announces to Jerusalem, 'Good news! You're saved. There will be peace. Your God is now King.'

ISAIAH 52:7

KILL THE MESSENGER?

The Big Breakfast

Being a messenger can be a nasty job. The practice of killing the bringer of bad news dates all the way back to biblical times (see 2 Samuel 1:15). Kings would sit in their castles waiting for someone to come over the hill: have we won our battle? Who has been killed? No wonder the Bible talks about how wonderful the messenger is when he brings good news!

Christians are the people of the gospel, the good news. Over the next five days we're going to think about what the good news about Jesus really is. And let's not forget that Jesus got killed too: his news wasn't good for everyone…

Just a few weeks ago I heard that I'm going to be a dad. Then, last week, I heard it was going to be twins! That was really good news, but boy, does it mean my life is going to change! News has that effect on you: if it didn't signal that something new and different was happening, it wouldn't be news. One of the interesting things about Christianity is that if you ask 10 people why they became Christians, you'll probably get 10 different answers. That's OK: God is good news to all of us!

Continental

Are we a good-news people to our world or a bad-news people?

Coffee

Think of three words that sum up what has been good news to you about being a Christian. If you have a pen handy, why not write them down in the space here:

Orange Juice

The Lord's Spirit has come to me, because he has chosen me to tell the good news to the poor. The Lord has sent me to announce freedom for prisoners, to give sight to the blind, to free everyone who suffers …

LUKE 4:18

THE GOOD NEWS MANIFESTO

The Big Breakfast

If you've been reading through this book, you'll have noticed that this passage has been quoted once already. Well, OK, I admit it, I am passionate about these few lines of Scripture.

This is the moment when Jesus brought both good and bad news to the people of Israel. Good news: God's salvation is available to everyone, no matter who they are. Bad news: that means that those who claim to hand out God's grace on his behalf are now out of a job.

This is the key to the good news of Jesus: whatever God has for us, it's up for grabs to anyone who wants it. This is revolutionary stuff: Jesus' good news was for all the people who couldn't get into the Temple in Jerusalem – the poor couldn't afford a sacrifice, those with disabilities were considered unclean and the prisoners … well, they speak for themselves. Thank you, Jesus!

Continental

Good news for the poor: what does that mean for the rich?

Coffee

What are the things that make you poor, a prisoner, blind? Say to yourself, 'If I turn to him, nothing can keep me from God, nothing can keep God from me.'

Orange Juice

After John was arrested, Jesus went to Galilee and told the good news that comes from God. He said, 'The time has come! God's kingdom will soon be here. Turn back to God and believe the good news!'   **MARK 1:14–15**

NEWS OF THE KINGDOM

The Big Breakfast

Jesus talks a lot about the Kingdom of God. Nobody ever knew exactly what he was talking about, but that was all part of the plan. Often when we think of the Kingdom, we think of heaven as a place in the future, but here Jesus says that the Kingdom is near ('upon you' is the best translation). The news that we have is that God is breaking into this world, that he's not some far-off, distant God who has just made the world and then gone for a fag. Jesus himself is a sign that God is close: God was willing to become like us in order to get the message across. Now that is good news!

But then we get this word 'repent', which literally means 'turn around'. The news about God's in-breaking Kingdom means that things have got to change: not just for the power-brokers, as Jesus has already said, but for all of us. Things can never be the same again. Once God calls us, we need to respond. He doesn't ask us to be perfect, but he does ask us to turn around and face him. If we move, we move towards him, and the closer we get to him, the more our lives are shown up in the light. We have to decide whether we want all that stuff to be shown up.

Continental

'If you have behaved badly, repent … On no account brood over your wrongdoing. Rolling in the muck is not the best way of getting clean' (Aldous Huxley).

Coffee

If Jesus came to visit you tomorrow, what would you want to do to get ready? Talk to God about it.

Orange Juice

I am not ashamed of the gospel, because it is the power of God for the salvation of everyone who believes.

ROMANS 1:16 NIV

POWER!

The Big Breakfast

Why would anybody be ashamed of the gospel? Well, we all know the answer to that question. Most of us will have found ourselves in a position where it's much easier to keep quiet than to admit that we are Christians. I'm supposed to be a 'professional' Christian, but there are still parties I go to where I just want to enjoy myself and not feel like I'm God's ambassador all the time. 'Ashamed' might be a bit strong, but 'embarrassed' – maybe that's more like it.

So why shouldn't I be ashamed? Because this gospel – this good news – is that God is powerful. 'Yeah, yeah,' I hear you say. 'So what? I know that – he wouldn't exactly be God if he wasn't, would he?' Well, that's true, but we don't generally live as if it were true.

And what's amazing about this statement is that the power of God comes from the good news and not the other way around. God's work through Jesus in saving us is the most powerful force in the universe, so grab hold and prepare for a ride!

Continental

'I'm not ashamed of the gospel, I'm not ashamed of the one I love,' sings Martin Smith. What about you?

Coffee

'May God shield me,/ May God fill me,/ May God keep me,/ May God watch me./ May God bring me/ To the land of peace,/ To the country of the King,/ To the peace of eternity' (ancient Celtic prayer).

Orange Juice

Then he told them: 'Go into all the world and preach the good news to all creation.'

MARK 16:15 NIV

The Big Breakfast

We've seen what the good news means to us as people, but what about the rest of the creation? We've seen that God cares about all kinds of people, that the good news is about 'justice and not just us', but what about the rest of the universe?

We don't often remember that God wants to bring the whole of creation round to his way of thinking, because it's all 'fallen' and in need of God's good news. This command of Jesus is scary on a number of counts: firstly, Jesus asks us to take responsibility for the whole world, and secondly, the whole world really is *the whole world*. Christians have often been at best apathetic about Green issues, but Jesus wants us to be good news to our rivers and rainforests as well as our poor and oppressed.

Continental

'Preach the gospel to all the world, and use words if necessary' (St Francis of Assisi).

Coffee

'I arise today/ Through the strength of heaven:/ Light of sun,/ Radiance of moon,/ Splendour of fire,/ Speed of lightning,/ Swiftness of wind,/ Depth of sea,/ Stability of earth,/ Firmness of rock' (ancient Irish prayer).

Orange Juice

But the chief priests ... were angry when they ... heard the children shouting praises to the Son of David ... Jesus answered. 'Don't you know that the Scriptures say, "Children and infants will sing praises"?'

MATTHEW 21:15-16

THE POWER OF WORDS

The Big Breakfast

For the next 10 readings I'm going to have a look at the Easter story, not from the point of view of the story itself or its observers, but from the perspective of Jesus' own words. Some of Jesus' words at this time are famous, while others are not. What is for sure is that you will see things a little differently over the next few days.

It's a beautiful scene: Jesus arrives at the Temple, surrounded by his disciples. Of course, the children don't fit in – this is a religious building! The priests are absolutely furious because these children are making a noise in their beloved Temple, but even worse, they are uttering blasphemy!

I can see the smile of Jesus as he responds to the priests. It is undoubtedly a neglected theme of the Bible that when adults refuse to listen to God, he just moves on to the next generation (see, for example, Gideon, Samuel, David and many others).

Continental

When churches used an image of Jesus similar to the famous picture of the South American revolutionary Che Guevara, with the punchline, 'JESUS: meek, mild. As if', there was a huge outcry. Why?

Coffee

These priests had somehow become fossilized over the years, but revival can start with the young. Talk to God about your own religious tradition and ask him to shake it up, if needs be.

Orange Juice
Jesus entered the temple area and drove out all who were buying and selling there … 'It is written,' he said to them, 'my house will be called a house of prayer, but you are making it a "den of robbers"'. *MATTHEW 21:12–13 NIV*

SPEAK OUT!

The Big Breakfast
This is one of those famous scenes that linger in the subconscious of our nation, although ask someone what it was about, and people often go quiet. No, the Temple wasn't an early shopping mall. In fact, the priests had come up with a groovy way of making money. OK, you have to come here to sacrifice an animal, but we won't let you bring your own: you must buy one of ours! Then, in order to buy one, you'll have to use our special Temple money! And, of course, we get to set the exchange rate!

Even Microsoft hasn't got that kind of monopoly. Jesus wasn't bothered by all the people hanging around in the Temple courts (maybe a bit like the church car park, or a huge foyer); he was bothered that they were being exploited by the ones who were supposed to be bringing them close to God. No wonder Jesus said what he said; he was mad!

Imagine spending three years trying to bring God close to the common people, and when you get to the place where people come to meet him, they have to lose the shirts from their backs to do so … Well, wouldn't you be upset?

Continental
'Justice is truth in action' (Benjamin Disraeli).

Coffee
If there is an injustice that you are angry about, bring this to God. If money and possessions are more important to you than prayer, take time to talk to God about it.

Orange Juice

Then he said to the servants, 'It is time for the wedding banquet, and the invited guests don't deserve to come. Go out to the street corners and tell everyone you meet to come to the banquet.'

MATTHEW 22:8–9

THE WRONG GUESTS

The Big Breakfast

You probably know this story, but did you know that Jesus told it just before he died? Jesus tells a story of a rich man having a party and, when he invites his friends, they don't seem to be all that bothered. In fact, they've all got something better to do. So he invites whoever will come, whatever they look (or smell) like.

Many of Jesus' stories at this time are thinly veiled threats against the Jewish leaders. Jesus is saying to them that God has invited them to THE wedding banquet, and they don't seem bothered about it. Perhaps they think that the places at the table almost belong to them: after all, they've been friends of the old man for so long, who else is he going to invite? Certainly not the dirty old Gentiles (non-Jews).

YOU SAID, 'WE'RE JEWS, WE'RE SAFE.' OUR SURVEY SAID, 'UH-UH!' WRONG! YOUR PLACES AT THE TABLE HAVE NOW BEEN TAKEN BY THE VERY PEOPLE YOU DESPISE THE MOST. GOODBYE, CHILDREN OF ISRAEL, YOU'VE MISSED YOUR PRIZE! [CAMERA MOVES TO BEAMING WINNERS, A BUNCH OF SMELLY OUTCASTS.]

Continental

Jesus once told a story with a similar message: a religious leader who was proud of his holy office was less likely to get into the Kingdom of God than a sinner who knew how much he needed Jesus (Luke 18:10–14). Watch out!

Coffee

Humility is an unfashionable virtue nowadays. Imagine you are one of the outcasts at the meal. What would you want to say to the host?

Orange Juice

Love the Lord your God with all your heart, soul, and mind. This is the first and most important commandment. The second most important commandment is like this one. And it is, 'Love others as much as you love yourself.'

MATTHEW 22:37–39

THE BIG ONE

The Big Breakfast

Which is the greatest commandment? To us, Jesus' answer to this question is so obvious, it hardly seems worth asking. However, go to many churches and you'll see the point. I have had the privilege of visiting many churches over the last 10 years, and nearly all of them have one thing in common: they eat people.

Somewhere along the line a church becomes an entity in itself, demanding all our energies and commitment. We lose sight of why we started in the first place: we have to keep feeding this machine. We have to find more gifted people to do this and that, we need more members, and on it goes, until – if God is gracious – somebody says, 'What are we doing all this for?' And then – if God is even more gracious – we hear the Holy Spirit saying one word: 'Love'.

I suspect that the Jewish authorities would have talked about the need to keep ritually clean and to honour God by religiously 'not getting into trouble'. Love breaks all that down. Love destroys the machine because it forces us to give our lives to God and to the service of others. Love destroys religion because it focuses on our heart-to-heart relationship with God. In this way, love conquers all.

Continental

'Love bade me welcome; yet my soul drew back,/ Guilty of dust and sin./ But quick-eyed love, observing me grow slack /From my first entrance in/ Drew nearer to me, sweetly questioning/ If I lacked anything' (George Herbert).

Coffee

Take time to meditate (think a bit) on either the Bible passage or the poem extract above.

Orange Juice

Jerusalem, Jerusalem! Your people have killed the prophets and have stoned the messengers who were sent to you. I have often wanted to gather your people, as a hen gathers her chicks under her wings. But you wouldn't let me.

MATTHEW 23:37

THE HEART OF GOD

The Big Breakfast

Shock-horror tabloid headline: 'GOD'S A WOMAN!' I've never been into the whole argument of God's gender, because to me it's like asking the gender of the universe.

OK, forget that stuff and think about Jesus, coming over the hill from Bethany, and this overwhelming passion ... well ... overwhelming him. This is beyond football, beyond Leonardo di Caprio, this is God's powerful love. He speaks to the city with such longing and tenderness that I can only imagine all these roughneck disciples suddenly finding their sandals to be of great interest. Healing, we can cope with, even raising the dead, but crying – no way!

Jesus knew what was about to happen, but he wasn't crying for himself; he was crying for all that was to come. There were people alive in Jerusalem who would live to see the city ransacked and the Temple destroyed less than 40 years later. I see this moment as being just as poignant as that in the Garden of Gethsemane. Jesus is saying to the city, 'If only you would turn back to God, none of us would have to go through what's going to happen.'

Continental

God longs to be as close to you as a mother is to her children. Cool, huh?

Coffee

Ask God to give you a little of his heart for where you live.

Orange Juice
The king will answer, 'Whenever you did it for any of my people, no matter how unimportant they seemed, you did it for me.'

MATTHEW 25:40

 SERVING JESUS

 ### The Big Breakfast
Matthew 25 should carry a health warning: 'Do not read this chapter if you want your life to stay the same.' After reading this chapter you have two choices: carry on living your life, being a bit 'spiritual', maybe even going to church, and end up on the scrapheap; or step outside your boundaries and go and serve Jesus.

That's one of the problems with so much of today's spirituality, Christian and not: fundamentally, it's a kind of God-induced therapy, with the sole aim of helping ME sort out MY problems and – if I'm lucky – helping ME become a better person (whatever that means!).

There's always been a tension in the church about this passage, because it seems to go against the whole 'God loves you and all you need is faith and you'll be saved' message, which I totally agree with. But I *also* agree with James: 'You have faith, show me it. I'll show you my faith by how my life has been changed' (my version of James 2:18). There's no getting round this: if you're a Christian and your life isn't different for it, something's wrong. One of the ways Jesus gives us to check on our own changed-ness is this chapter. When we serve the poor, we serve him.

 ### Continental
'If a man be gracious and courteous to strangers, it shows he is a citizen of the world' (Francis Bacon).

 ### Coffee
Is there someone you know who you need to serve as if they were Jesus?

Orange Juice

During the meal Jesus took some bread in his hands. He blessed the bread and broke it. Then he gave it to his disciples and said, 'Take this and eat it. This is my body.'

MATTHEW 26:26

THE WORDS OF GRACE

The Big Breakfast

The power of this moment still gets me, as does the stupidity of the disciples. Jesus has been living with the knowledge that this is the time for his death for many days (probably months), and he knows that there is a traitor in their midst. Holding up the Passover bread, he reminds the disciples of when the children of Israel were in so much of a hurry to escape Egypt that they had to make unleavened bread. They are thinking of that day, many centuries before, when God saved his people, and then Jesus says it: 'This is my body.'

Woah. I don't think they got it even then. They knew Jesus was special, so how could he die? That just didn't fit in with the plan. Here he was, saying what? That what he was about to do was as important as what Moses did? That he was going to save an entire people for God? They were only having dinner!

Continental

The Lord's Supper is one of the few things that Jesus asked us to do regularly. Why do you think it's so important?

Coffee

Think for a bit about each of these different meanings: *Eucharist:* thanksgiving to God for Jesus' death for our salvation, *Communion:* relationship with God and with each other, *The Lord's Supper:* remembering Jesus' life, death and resurrection, *The Mass:* feeding us and sending us out to serve God in the world. Bet you never knew there was so much in it!

Orange Juice
Jesus knelt with his face to the ground and prayed, 'My Father, if it is possible, don't make me suffer by making me drink from this cup. But do what you want, and not what I want.'

MATTHEW 26:39

ALONE

The Big Breakfast
If you've ever seen the musical *Jesus Christ Superstar* you'll know that this scene is the real heart of the piece, not the dodgy disco title track. For me, it perfectly encapsulates Jesus' pain that God had put him in this inescapable position, and yet his willingness to obey his Father, even when he couldn't completely see the way forward. It's the night before his arrest, and Jesus is in the Garden of Gethsemane begging God for a way out of what is about to happen.

Maybe we have this idea that Jesus approached his own torture and slow death with a kind of secret pleasure, knowing that he was going to get his own back on his enemies when – ta-da! – he rose from the dead. I don't think so. As much as the cross, Gethsemane tells us the price Jesus was willing to pay for us. He's surrounded by his closest friends and allies, all asleep, and he has to face this night alone.

There is no equivalent. I'm sitting here at my computer trying to think of a nice modern-day analogy, but there just isn't one.

Thank you, Jesus.

Continental
Jesus had many options open to him that night: he could have begged Judas not to betray him, he could have run away, he could have died defending himself, he could have prepared a brilliant defence for Pilate. What would you have done?

Coffee
Is there an area in your life where you need to say to God, 'But do what you want, and not what I want'?

Orange Juice

Pilate asked him, 'Don't you hear what crimes they say you have done?' But Jesus did not say anything, and the governor was greatly amazed.

MATTHEW 27:13–14

SILENCE IS GOLDEN

The Big Breakfast

Jesus was an amazing guy. He was so full of wisdom, and frequently his words silenced his critics. Yet now, at the precise moment where his words could save him, Jesus says nothing. I know this reading is a bit of a cheat, seeing as we were meant to be looking at things Jesus said, but at this point his silence is as important as his words. Was he silent like a man defeated, awaiting his fate? Or was his the silence of a defiant schoolboy, chin up and staring hard to prevent the tears of anger? We'll never know for sure, but I think Jesus' silence reflected his knowledge that, in his own bitter-sweet words, 'It is finished.'

Jesus had decided the night before that he was willing to die for his Father. In a funny way, I wonder if he was impatient to get the 'formal' proceedings over and done with. As the guards beat him and stole his clothes, he was at peace.

In many ways, this silence *was* defiance: Jesus was not going to get trapped into some petty argument or a feeble attempt to beg for mercy. He was able to rise above the chaos that surrounded him as he was dragged from pillar to post, because he knew his destiny and was willing to trust God.

Continental

There is a time for speaking and a time for silence. Is there something that you need to say that you haven't said so far? Is there something you need *not* to say?

Coffee

Can you make room in your life for silence? If you have never spent time in silence before, you will find it agonizing, but try to give yourself five minutes to just sit in silence. When the early monastics said, 'Go to your cell, it will teach you everything,' they were talking about silence.

Orange Juice
Go to the people of all nations and make them my disciples. Baptize them in the name of the Father, the Son, and the Holy Spirit, and teach them to do everything I have told you.   *MATTHEW 28:19-20*

FAMOUS LAST WORDS

The Big Breakfast
If you've been following through on this series, you'll have noticed that I've missed out the important stuff. Well, that's true, but I've only done that because it's the stuff you know so well. I wanted to look at the bits that surround the famous words and stories. But here's a famous bit.

I have a friend who talks about this passage all the time, and he always begins by asking the same question: 'In the Greek, one of the verbs in the main sentence ('go', 'make', 'baptize', 'teach') is the main command Jesus gave, while the others are more like, 'and while you're doing that one, you should do these three as well ...' Which one is it?' Everybody says 'go', when in fact the main verb in the sentence is 'make'.

This tells us something important about Jesus, because to me the word 'disciple' says that being a Christian is a lifetime thing, so much more than 'becoming a Christian'. That's just the beginning of a lifelong adventure!

Continental
Are you merely a convert or are you a disciple?

Coffee
Is there someone you know well who you can pray for today, that they become a disciple of Jesus? They might be a Christian or not. As you pray, remember that making disciples is our job, given to us by Jesus.

Orange Juice

Yet a time is coming and has now come when the true worshippers will worship the Father in spirit and in truth, for they are the kind of worshippers the Father seeks.

JOHN 4:23 NIV

ME – A WORSHIPPER?

The Big Breakfast

As we come to the end of this book, I realize there's something I have taken for granted. Something that's so obvious that it seems an insult to mention it to you: Jesus. I hope by reading this book your mind will have been expanded, and perhaps a few dark corners of the Bible will have been illuminated, if only a little, and only for a little while.

Yet my chief aim in this book, as in my life, is to help others to learn to love and follow my Lord Jesus. These next five days give me a great opportunity to just shout *JESUS!!!!* really loud, and hopefully you'll get the idea.

Anyone who loves and follows Jesus is a worshipper, but Jesus helped us to understand worship a little better, using the two words 'spirit' and 'truth'. Sometimes we try to separate these two out, so we have a 'spirit' time (normally singing), followed by a 'truth' time (normally somebody talking for a very long time). But real worship involves both the mind and the spirit: it can't be just spiritual communion, nor just knowledge, but when both are in place, then you've got it.

Continental

'The worship of God is not a rule of safety – it is an adventure of the spirit, a flight after the unattainable' (A. N. Whitehead).

Coffee

Read the verse above a few times and let the words sink into you, asking God to speak to you through them. Which words stick out to you? Focus on them and talk to God about what they mean to you.

Orange Juice
Dear friends, God is good. So I beg you to offer your bodies to him as a living sacrifice, pure and pleasing. That's the most sensible way to serve God.

ROMANS 12:1

The Big Breakfast
Don't worry about today's title – I haven't suddenly gone all fitness-crazed on you. In fact, I have to say that I think today's body-fascism is one of the most powerful strongholds of the enemy in the West today. No, I'm talking about worshipping God with our bodies. And that doesn't mean liturgical dance or shaking violently either.

If we had a chance to ask God what way he preferred to be worshipped, I suspect he would say, 'With your lives.' I can't imagine anything pleasing God more than people who love him so much that they will do anything for him. As someone with a slightly sick sense of humour once said, the problem with living sacrifices is that they have a tendency to crawl off the altar. Those that stay there are therefore even more precious to God our Father.

Worship is so often nowadays connected with singing the right songs and going to the right conferences: let's leave all that behind and reach out after Jesus, living in a way that will have people turning their heads and knowing that he really does exist.

Continental
'Worship is the submission of all our nature to God. It is the quickening of conscience by his holiness, the nourishment of the mind with his truth, the purifying of the imagination by his beauty, the opening of the heart to his love, the surrender of the will to his purpose' (William Temple).

Coffee
Read through the William Temple quote on this page a few times, until you have fully understood each clause and are ready to ask God that it be true of you.

Orange Juice
We bring nothing at birth; we take nothing with us at death. The LORD alone gives and takes. Praise the name of the LORD!

JOB 1:21

IN SICKNESS AND IN HEALTH

The Big Breakfast
Recently I heard a terrible story about a woman from the Dangerous Sports Club who had broken her pelvis being thrown out of a medieval catapult built by her boyfriend. The newsreaders that were trying to convey this story to me just couldn't do it: their laughter got the better of them. It wasn't that this lady's pain wasn't real, it was just that the situation had reached comic proportions: TV cameras were there to record the abject failure (or was it success?) of this latest attempt to do something stupid.

Job's story has something of the comically tragic about it: it's so bad that you have to smile at the guy. It's probably some biological defence mechanism: we just can't help being happy that it's not us! Yet Job had something that was perhaps more precious than all that he lost: a faithful heart. That's special.

I had a friend at college who told me that he had decided not to be a Christian because God hadn't provided him with good enough friends. Pardon? Aren't you getting God and a mail-order catalogue a bit mixed up here? Still, that's how it is with many Christians. As long as everything is OK, I'll worship you, Lord. But as soon as anything goes wrong, you're out the door and I'll be trying out the old Feng Shui.

Continental
'Faithfulness in little things is a big thing' (Chrysostom).

Coffee
If you can, try writing down something that might look a bit like a psalm. Remember that the psalms in the Bible included both complaint and praise together, verse by verse: don't feel ashamed of letting your bad feelings out along with your praise.

Orange Juice

Be joyful and sing as you come in to worship the LORD!

PSALM 100:2

IF MUSIC BE THE FOOD OF LOVE ...

The Big Breakfast

Think of a piece of music that makes you *feel* something. I know that a few of you won't be able to do this because you're not into music, but you will surely know someone who is the opposite: music provides a constant soundtrack to their life. If you're unlucky, you might sit next to them on the bus, listening to that annoying *szztin szztin* sound coming out of their Walkman.

But when you stand looking out at the ocean or at the top of a hill, or look down a microscope at the wonders of a human cell, or marvel at the complexities of the human mind, and say, 'God made that!', the same is true of music. He needn't have bothered, we could have managed without it, but God wanted to make something that expressed beauty and emotion in a way that is beyond explanation, just as he is.

Music was made for the worship of God, and you forget it. You may think that music was made to get young girls drunk on a Friday night so not-so-young men can get them into bed, but it's not true: every note, every chord was created by him. So use it! And that goes for all the arts too ...

Continental

'Anyone who does not find [God] in his wonderful work of music is truly a clod and is not worthy to be called human!' (Martin Luther).

Coffee

Find time to play some music, read a good book, go to an art gallery – or do something else you enjoy that will help you to worship God.

Orange Juice

These people honour me with their lips, but their hearts are far from me. They worship me in vain; their teachings are but rules taught by men.

MARK 7:6-7 NIV

TRUTH AND SPIRIT

The Big Breakfast

This is the tough one. As Christians we walk a very fine line. We are called to worship God however we feel, yet we mustn't get into meaningless routine and ritual – which, let's face it, does tend to happen when we try to worship when our heart's not in it. It's obviously something that Jesus felt passionate about, because he talks quite a bit about it.

The key seems to be this both/and thing, which is really, really hard. Not enough truth, and you float off into the clouds in a haze of spiritual ecstasy (well, we can dream, can't we?); not enough spirit, and we crumble and die, but of course we do it with doctrinal purity. The only way out of this, as far as I can see, is Jesus.

Because Jesus is the source of the Spirit, and describes himself as the truth, if we want to worship God rightly, we need to completely immerse ourselves in the person of Jesus. Read the Gospels over and over again. If that's too hard, get hold of a copy of *The Book of God*, which contains the story of Jesus in an easier form. Do whatever you need to do in order to keep your worship alive. Jesus said it himself: 'If you know me, you know God.'

Continental

'The person who really knows God will worship him' (Seneca).

Coffee

Focus on Jesus in some way, either remembering a story about him or just conjuring up an image of him in your mind. Worship him now!